б

хронт

17724

COUNTRY REPORTER

COUNTRY REPORTER

David Foot

A Graham Tarrant Book
David & Charles
Newton Abbot   London

British Library Cataloguing in Publication Data
Foot, David, 1929–
    Country reporter.
    1. Great Britain. Journalism – Biographies
    I. Title
    070'.92'4

    ISBN 0–7153–9255–7

Printed in Great Britain
by Billlings & Sons   Worcester
for David & Charles Publishers plc
Brunel House   Newton Abbot   Devon

To Anne; to Clare and Sarah, James and Polly,
one of whom could even become a
third-generation journalist
in the family

Contents

Author's Note

This is above all an affectionate look-back on my craft in the days before newspaper high-tech and the cruel rent-boy syndrome of the more prying tabloids. Every big town and city had two evening papers. The reporters beat each other to the nearest phone box, and then shared a convivial pint. I'm sure journalism was more fun.

In my own small town of Yeovil in Somerset, there were, in addition to my own paper, three evenings vying eagerly for the sales. My colleagues taught me to be competitive, news-conscious and, I trust, good natured. They helped with a suspect shorthand outline – and showed me how to land a story in London. The warm regard I had for my old weekly, the *Western Gazette*, whatever the frustrations at the time, still comes through, I hope. The warm-hearted world of 'Cherry', 'Buzz' and 'Rowly' were a valuable part of my education.

The book is very much a romantic odyssey, written in gratitude. My grandfather, Jack, was really my mentor and I think he forgave me for not becoming a garage mechanic.

My thanks go to Graham Tarrant, who came up with the idea for the book and then gave me much encouragement; to my first publisher, the late Nigel Hollis, who before his untimely death kept giving me kindly prods; and to all my contemporaries from the reporters' and maligned subs' room.

D.F.

ONE

A New Suit

EXCITING JOB you've got, son. What do you like best of all?'
It became an irritating, recurrent question whenever I
flourished my thick greenhorn's notebook in readiness for
the latest parochial pronouncement from someone who really had
nothing worth conveying to our captive rural readership.

'Thursday night when the button is pressed.'

I'd leave it like that, vague and arcane – because Thursday
night, press night, was my romantic secret. It was a stealthy ritual
that unfailingly made me tingle. The feeling surged down past my
loins into my boots and then, almost in the same movement, back
up into a head that was swimming with exhilaration. What went on,
down in the machine room, was for me the distillation of a hundred
journalistic aspirations. I was simply mesmerised by the physical
presence of the presses, their sheer majesty and vibrating grandeur,
their pounding exertions as new lives were being created and safely
delivered.

There was so much more to transfix me in that throbbing technical
chamber: the visual complexities of the intertwining cylinders and
newly-cast stereo plates, the momentary glisten of wet ink on virgin
paper, the intricate cuts and folds. . .

Earlier in the day I'd seen the big lorry back into the bay and unload
the reels of newsprint, like giant toilet rolls, with five miles of paper
on each one. And now here, at the touch of a podgy, ink-stained
finger, the rotary presses were beginning to hum and revolve, and
those miles of newsprint to thread their way on the first part of the
journey to tomorrow's doorstep.

The men in the machine room always seemed to have the
jovial, perspiring faces and well-fleshed features of sailors from the
engine room. When one of them caught me peeping at the magic of

9

the operation, he'd chortle: 'Han't killed off the mayor be mistake, have'ee Matt? Too late to chip now.'

And as he said it, the second button would be pressed – for increased speed from the roaring rotaries. The language from the brawny operators, bawled above the noise, always added to the esoteric delights. 'Is them plates kissin' the paper nicely, Wilf?'

There was always the apparently token glance at the first of the papers as they came off the press, to make sure there were no tears or smudges, and then the look of unspoken satisfaction.

Not much more than eighteen months in the job so far. But already I'd cycled miles in the service of my profession on a faithful three-speed, had knocked on many friendly and unfriendly doors, dutifully learned to rattle out the acceptable clichés, courted with libel, sunk pints of strong local brew in the pretences of adulthood, loved and lost a libidinous waitress, and interviewed a future prime minister. Not bad. Especially as I was also still uncynical enough to become hypnotically immobilised within sight and sound of the rolling presses.

I made my way back to the reporters' room, now deserted. It smelt of stale fags and wet galley proofs. Untidy stacks of spent notebooks, chronicling the monumental ordinariness of a thousand West Country parish pumps, littered the tables and window ledges. The last week's compounded reports of courts and councils were, even as I contemplated the thought, threading their predestined passage through and around the cylinders down below. It brought home to me the odd ephemera of my emergent working life.

The door opened a foot and the editor peeped in. He was surprised to see me still there. 'Working late, I see. That's good. Remember, young man, that in a few years' time after your National Service, there may be one or two district men's jobs going. That would appeal to you, wouldn't it?'

'Yes,' I said. I thought of dear old Bill, long the local reporter at Crewkerne, who by much cunning and administrative skill was now able to take his favourite seat in the George Hotel at noon each day, waiting for the meticulously briefed town contacts to arrive with their information or, more often, already compiled reports. If Bill's proffered copy was occasionally beer-stained, no-one ever seemed to notice.

'Let me see, now, didn't you come from Yeovil School?'

I nodded, warily.

Affected by the relief of seeing another week's paper out of the way, the editor had remained more cordial to me than he had ever been before. 'A strange little story came in from there late this afternoon. It appears that one of the sixth formers fooled the whole school. He put on a moustache and a white coat and claimed to be the visiting medical officer. Do you know, he examined a hundred or so boys and no-one was any the wiser. Yes, very strange.'

'Gosh!' I said, partly in admiration at the daring of the imposter, and partly in instant contemplation of supplementary earnings.

'Of course, we didn't use it. Oh dear me, no! I understand this young fellow got rather above himself and was proposing to examine the two female members of staff next. Oh dear me, – not our line of country at all, I'm glad to say.'

It was a sentiment, of sturdy puritan zeal, hardly likely to be shared by one or two lurid Sundays I could immediately think of.

I hadn't been back to my old grammar school for those past eighteen months. Now perhaps was the time. Not strictly an academic return, of course. More, this search for the phantom medic, a symbol. It would signal for me, as part of my foraging, formative, wide-eyed years, the conclusion of an unpredictable rounded tour.

*   *   *

The headmaster's study had a distinctive smell – on the week I started at my town grammar school and now, on the day I was about to leave in 1946. It was a mixture of cabbage water, which wafted along from the kitchens past the assembly hall in the front, and the escapes from a score of bunsen burners, snaking their noxious way from the chemistry lab at the back.

'Ah yes, just a quick word before you leave for good, em –'

'Fouracre, sir.'

'Yes, Fouracre. I hope it's been a fruitful residence for you over the past five years and that you feel you have benefited, shall we say, intellectually.'

The Head was an English scholar. He clipped and chiselled and fashioned his words with an affectionate precision. He had written books with F.R. Leavis; it was that kind of academic grandeur. On his desk was stacked a flawlessly symmetrical pile of *News-letters*, containing the worthy sentiments of Commander Sir Stephen King-Hall, offered each week as a supposed stimulating alternative to the more orthodox territory of religious instruction.

This eager, excited, acned sixth former summoned up unfamiliar powers of resourcefulness as he braced himself for scholastic departure.

'I wondered, sir, if I might leave a couple of days early – Tuesday instead of Thursday. There is probably nothing much for me to do here. And . . . I'd . . . like to – '

'See the Indians at Taunton?'

Till then, I had never thought him in any sense a cricketing man. He had these thick, book-wormy glasses, a pallid, lugubrious face verging on the cod-like features of a younger and rather taller Leslie Henson, and he appeared to glide round, ever tugging at his gown, in vague introspection. He was gentle and remote: and we never saw him on match days.

'Let me see, Fouracre, you've been in the 1st XI this season, haven't you?'

'And last, sir.'

'Have you made many runs?'

'I got 16 at Dorchester when we were up against it, sir.'

'Was that your top score?' he asked in a tone which I felt was unreasonably dismissive.

'Well, no sir. I also got 16 when we played Huish's on the county ground at Taunton. Mr Sparks gave me run-out and afterwards told me he'd made a mistake.'

The headmaster clearly disapproved of superficial conversation. 'Did you stay on for a whole year in the sixth form just to play cricket?' I fancied he was close to adding that, considering my token batmanship, I'd have been advised to leave a year earlier. He had the good grace to remain silent.

'No, sir. I needed another credit for matriculation. So I took my English again.' I knew immediately it was the wrong thing to say.

'Do I assume that English is not one of your better subjects?'

'It's my best, sir,' I blurted out. 'But I took so long on my essay last year that I never got round to the grammar.' I thought I detected the flicker of a smile behind those heavy glasses. Now it was time for me to toady, to make my predetermined statement of civilised farewell.

'Enjoyed your book, sir. I got it out of the Yeovil library. Very good it was, sir.'

'Which of my books was that, Fouracre?' It wasn't in any way a haughty put-down. I played safe. 'I think it's your latest – *Between The Lines Or How To Read A Newspaper*.'

'Yes, that one. It's a rather long title, I fear.'

My longest previous, in fact my only, dialogue with the head-master had been twenty seconds of relative badinage at the time of the School's mock election, when I had produced some pretty puer-ile satirical couplets as self-appointed publicist for the Labour Party. It was hard for a sensitive schoolboy not to be swept up and carried along by the unleashed tide of political feeling just after the war. It was the perfect time to be an emotional socialist.

The Head was fidgeting with some papers and I knew it would soon be time to go. But I was conscious of the psychological shifting of balance and lessening of inhibition that comes with leaving school. 'You don't seem to think much of the Press, sir.'

It was his hobby horse and he treated me to a few of his more scathing views. They were mostly to do with selectivity, propaganda and what he saw as the unforgiveable dispensing of trivia and pap. He listed his indictments in a quiet, withering way. The argument was inclined to be above my head but I suspected he had some valid points.

The vehemence of his words took me by surprise; I knew at once I shouldn't have tried to curry favour with what was basically an insincere adolescent compliment.

'Now I must really see the next boy. Leave us a day or so early if you wish to. And yes, I should have asked you this, what are you planning to do with your life now that you have decided to reject Higher School Certificate and perhaps university?'

It was a difficult moment for me. I felt the eminently rational Stephen King-Hall might have been better suited to handle the obvi-ous hiatus of unease. I gulped and with a voice of affected challenge, lacking in conviction, I said 'I'm going to be a journalist, sir.' There was a tangible silence. The headmaster walked towards the door and held it open. 'Yes, well. . .yes. Good luck, Fouracre – I'm sure you will do very well.' It was the kind of pay-off that beggared interpre-tation.

Still a nice man, I thought. Yet what did an ivory-tower academic really know about newspapers and printer's ink? (I'd already acquired all the romantic jargon.) That book of his might make a well-argued paper, to be delivered to some esoteric group of cloistered fogies. But what did he understand about human interest stories, about chasing to phone boxes to beat deadlines and competitors?

That night I went home and confided in my grandfather, as I always did. He'd long been one of my heroes: a one-time gamekeeper with a thirst so indiscreet that whenever he was given a gold half-sovereign for 'beating' at a Boxing Day or bank holiday shoot, he had spent it all by the time he was led home by his faithful spaniel. He could read with great difficulty but had the big family Bible out on the table every evening. He claimed that he had read the Good Book from cover to cover three times and I believed him. I was transfixed as I watched him slowly run his engrained fingernail along each line. It was for him a laborious but rewarding process. Sarah, his sweet-natured wife, would sit in silence at the side of the hearth, bravely bearing the constant pain of acute rheumatism she had suffered for thirty years. My grandfather would fetch her long, lethal looking bunches of stinging nettles, the stems and leaves bristling with the toxic needles. She would rub the nettles up and down her frail arms and around the warped knuckles of her hands, in an effort to offset the pain. She was down to five stone and a brown shawl hung loosely over the protruding bones and wrinkled features. Often she winced with the pain but never once did I hear her complain.

My grandfather prepared the food, which consisted mainly of a breakfast of Quaker Oats, prepared with unwavering ritual overnight. He measured the oats out and added a generous dab of butter. It was the perfect meal, he told me with the convictions of a rustic chef, to keep out the cold and act as a laxative. The breakfast components never changed. As a young man he was a fine athlete and ran the eighteen miles from his home near Dorchester to Sherborne Castle where Sarah was in service. Then, after a night's innocent courting below stairs, he would run home again. He had to be up at six o'clock next morning. I heard him often described as the best gamekeeper in Dorset; he came from a long line of them and the loyalties and skills of one descendant were movingly recorded on a tombstone, at the instigation of the lord of the manor, in Upcerne churchyard. My grandfather's accuracy with a gun was legendary. Such precision of aim was still evident in late life as he sat at the table, leaned to his left and spat into the fire – always to my astonishment missing the bars and reaching the blackened hunk of apple wood with a triumphant hiss.

The tablecloth was a jigsaw arrangement of the past week's *News Chronicles*. I first read the distinctive imagery of my earliest newspaper idols, Robert Lynd and Ian Mackay, between the soggy stains of spilt Quaker Oats.

It was, I am sure, a disappointment to him when I first said what I wanted to do with my working life. 'Ought to be a car mechanic, me son. That's a real job. Good money. Always be them motor cars about.'

He'd grown up through the Ford revolution. The Tin Lizzie had been for him a glamorous, unattainable wonder. Even now, in 1946, whenever there were cars in the road, he would hobble to the window and survey them with the doting eyes of a schoolboy. The internal combustion engine remained a mystery. Yet those who understood its intricacies and enthusiastically dirtied their hands on a car's remedial necessities were to him cleverer than solicitors or country parsons.

'You be goin' to work for the *News Chronicle*, then. Will I be seen' yur name in it when I do have me breakfast?'

I smiled and refrained from proud boasts. For the time being, the *Western Gazette* seemed a bit of a let-down.

I walked out of his little estate-cottage, alongside the pub and opposite my own thatched home. Dad had also worked on the estate up to the war, as a woodman. Mother had met him when she was a housemaid at the Big House. That evening, on the day I left school, I pondered for the first time on the way the village was changing. East Coker tugged at me emotionally. Without being able to articulate the sensation, I knew that postwar attitudes were different, more defiant. The hierarchical levels were disappearing. Village boys were back from the fighting in France and Italy, looking older and more cynical: saying radical things their fathers would never have dreamed of saying.

The ironmonger's van, laden like Mother Courage's canteen, pulled up outside my home and I was jerked out of my reverie. My mother had heard it and was already coming down the path, between the hollyhocks, with her empty paraffin can – needed for the oil lamp which still served as our only lighting in the oak-beamed living room – and carrying with greater difficulty the cumbersome wireless accumulator that had to be recharged.

A shabby Morris 7, miraculously revitalised after a wartime of enforced hibernation, grunted and spluttered its way past. But there were few signs of cars or emergent affluence, to coincide with the winning of a war. Cyclists arrived at the New Inn, offered a perfunctory wave and went into the public bar where the cider was accessible and the beer was cheaper. None of the villagers went into the lounge. That would have been considered altogether too grand a gesture and, worse, disloyal.

Suddenly I was consumed with an ingenuous surge of power. School belonged to the past. I was now a worker: more than that, I was a writer. It was no time to debate the disparity between journalism and so-called literature – to me they both dispensed words and conveyed emotions.

I'd start with my beloved village of East Coker. T.S. Eliot had written a whole poem about it after all – and I'd now write a whole article about him. J.B. Priestley had rhapsodized over its charms. William Dampier, the explorer, had been born here. And I would write about Charlie Mayo who had kept a pet raven and also played cricket for Somerset; of farmer Billy Richards, whose potent homemade cider consistently drew a bigger Sunday morning congregation than filled the pews in the parish church; of Fred and Jack, who could do everything from sweep the chimneys to castrate the squealing cats; of Don, the local schoolmaster's son, who wanted only to dance like Astaire. . .I'd let the readers know. And, at the top. . .By Matthew Fouracre. No, too stuffy. By MATT FOURACRE.

My hand was still resting on the peeling front gate of my grandfather's cottage, as my head spun with grandiose journalistic ideas. That little gate, split and unpainted since 1939, held mischievous memories for me. Hanging on it, the morning after the VE Day street party – when everyone had with indiscriminate joy linked arms to dance the horsey-horsey and okey-cokey and steal furtive kisses – had been a spent contraceptive.

'Look,' my pal Pete had said, 'a bloody frenchie on yer gran'fer's gate.'

I was just sixteen and hadn't yet used one. But the members of my particular form at school had long been experts on sexually related rubberware. One of our classmates would produce them at will from his wallet. They were an American brand and it was tacitly accepted that his mother had a prodigious regard for the GIs, stationed in his village during the war. He would proudly place a packet of three on his desk during the lunch hour and then delicately take out one French letter, placing his finger suggestively inside. We would crowd round, fascinated by the neatness of the packaging and the unspoken innuendoes that aroused rampant imaginations.

Next morning, before catching the stopper train from Hendford Halt to Taunton for the cricket, I cycled the four miles to Yeovil. I freewheeled down Middle Street and leaned my dropped handlebar machine rather recklessly against the plate-glass front of Messrs Bone & Flagg, high class gentlemen's outfitters. It was my second visit in

16

a fortnight. 'Ah, good morning, welcome back – you are still interested?'

The manager had materialised from behind the curtains of one of
the alcoves. His shop had a certain resilient well-heeled decadence
about it. It stood on its small-town dignity, with a whiff of moth balls
and of the kind of aura that goes with superior quality materials, and
an incongruous murmur of eau-de-Cologne. It made all those grey
demob suits look even more drab and misshapen on the war-weary
bodies outside.

'There it is, sir. A very fine suit. Well cut. And with a lot of
style. You are very fortunate to be able to have it straightaway.'

I saw it on the hanger. It was brown pinstripe, far more ambitious
than anything I had ever contemplated before. Indeed, it was my
first suit – apart from the obligatory school uniform. At six guineas,
it was twice as much as my parents had ever paid for me. The manager
had gone to pains on my last visit to tell me what a stroke of luck it
was, ideal for my first job. As I must know, cloth was in painfully
short supply and normally I might have to wait six or even nine
months. Then I might have to put up with only an approximation
of the pattern I had ordered. And linings, oh dear me yes, they were
another problem – they didn't come at the right time and that meant
more delays. 'Everyone had imagined things would be easier after the
war, sir, but well, we buy in bulk and hope for the best. Always very
personal attention here, sir, as I am sure you know.' He gave me a
warm look of sincerity.

He repeated: 'Yes, a very fine suit. And such a sad background.
As I believe I told you, the delightful person for whom we made it
has passed on. So we were left with it. I-I assume you'd like it.'

'Yes, please,' I said. I was beckoned to one of the alcoves to try
it on for a third if not fourth time. The manager hovered and I was
embarrassed as I kept catching his eye in the mirror. 'Blue eyes,' he
said with a confidentiality that made me uneasy, 'don't always go with
brown, of course. But I'm sure you can carry it off.' He chuckled with
a reassurance that seemed more sexual than managerial. There was a
meandering monologue about whether the trousers were a trifle too
baggy and it might be a good idea if he checked the inside-leg meas-
urements again. My instincts told me to discourage the operation and
I said I was satisfied.

I dressed again and as he wrapped the suit, I produced six one-
pound notes and six shillings in mint condition. 'Such a nuisance,
sir, but I do hope you have got the necessary coupons. We can't be

too careful,' said the manager. He had by now acquired a certain air of insouciance. From a used buff envelope given me by my mother, I took the loose, grubby, part-borrowed coupons. The clothing allocation had been cut to thirty-six coupons the previous September. Now a suit of clothes seemed to take most of them.

My day had been programmed, not least in the sartorial sense. I cycled back up the hill and went into the public conveniences. I put on my new suit; journalists didn't wear faded sports jackets and stained grey flannels. After rolling my discarded clothes into the wrapping paper, I squeezed the lot into the carrier fixed to my bicycle saddle and pedalled with preening good humour to Hendford Halt. I probably looked the best dressed sixteen-year-old ever to take a ride on the single track to Gimblett's Taunton.

It wasn't vanity. Like most village boys with a crippling inferiority complex, I was capable of masking my social shortcomings with an extrovert flourish. And I was inordinately proud of my new professional status.

GWR, five shillings and sevenpence return of hissing steam, had its own romance, of course. It didn't matter that the begrimed livery had faded to indeterminate design and that I had to stand in a crowded corridor each way. Much of the hour-long journey, through the buttercup cuttings, was for me an elongated daydream. My mother had dutifully prepared and folded in greaseproof paper my favourite blackcurrant jam sandwiches; they were my only diversion.

They used to say, long before Mr Beeching got to work, that the small, rattling run through Athelney and King Alfred country took you along the friendliest line in Britain. It was certainly the most informal. Sometimes after a long delay we'd look out of the window and see the driver helping a farmer hustle a few reluctant sheep along the platform. The farmer would throw a couple of rabbits up into the cab then as a reward.

It was very much a rural ride. There always seemed to be milk floats at Thorney and Kingsbury Halt, always peonies in bloom at Langport West, almost always a little girl up in the signal box with her father at Martock, where for some obscure reason the platforms didn't face each other. Durstan and Creech St Michael: it sounded so nice and civilised. And with cricket still to come.

Over the three days, Somerset, full of amiable and leathery faced old pros back from the war, beat the Indians by an innings. There was a bulging crowd, many of us sitting on the grass. During the lunch and tea breaks, I would walk in front of the small, elevated press box and, no doubt erroneously, put names to faces. I remember spying and pausing in awe of R.C. Robertson-Glasgow, contemplative, chin wedged in cupped palms. Later, to my dismay, I discovered he was nowhere near the ground.

But Bill Andrews was there – and so was Bertie Buse, bowling out the Indians between them before lunch for 64; in Bill's case, doing it in a borrowed pair of boots. I took a notebook, with Yeovil School's crest and motto, *Esse Quam Videri*, on the front cover and redundant Latin declensions on the opening pages. I turned the book round and started at the back, making notes each day: of an impressive newcomer, Micky Walford, in his Harlequin cap, taking a wonderful catch at deep square leg, just in front of me; of dashing, prince-like Asian athletes in the outfield. For the journey home on the third day, I had a seat and conscientiously I fashioned a five-hundred-word report of the match, followed by the full scoreboard. The handwriting was neat, the phrases inclining to purple on occasions. I thought seriously about submitting my considered piece to the *Western Gazette* but finally concluded, with some reluctance, that they would have their own experienced sports reporter squeezed in that press box of illustrious names, to describe an historic win. To my horror, I discovered that my new employers, one of the biggest weekly papers in the country and proud of being Somerset-based, considered the match worth just twelve lines of minuscule type.

It was no more than a fleeting frustration for a lad just out of school and on the point of bursting himself assuredly into print.

My postwar Coker was at the same time a sad and exciting place. It was sad that Ken, the village's opening bat, a gentle boy who I am sure had no hate for either the Germans or opposing fast bowlers, hadn't come back from the war. Nor had Charles, an Old Etonian, who I like to think for reasons of unwavering fellowship, never got beyond the rank of sergeant. A dozen or so from the parish didn't survive.

And I also missed the young evacuees, who had arrived from London with their chirpy, unfamiliar voices and dirty noses. They had shown us another culture, reminded us that it wasn't only the farm labourers who were poor.

The excitement was less easy to define. We had some guilt, whatever our politics, about the way Churchill, the war idol, had been kicked out of office. We knew we should be uneasy about the way the Yanks were caning us with their loan charges now that Lend-lease had ended. And we weren't quite sure what to make of this public school bloke, Attlee, who seemed altogether too mild-mannered and diffident after the brilliant bombast of Winnie. But Ernie Bevin was a bit different.

'Old Ernie. . .you can tell from the way he do talk. . .he's a Somerset lad. And a real bastard!'

'Wos mean? Why's he such a bastard, then?'

'Cos he han't got a father, tha's what. His mother weren't wed.'

That settled the argument. Illegitimacy had an acceptable ring to it, in the rebellious social spirit of the mid-Forties. Old attitudes were being openly questioned. Whether you read the *Daily Mirror* or the *New Statesman*, you were assured the world was going to be a better place. That meant Britain. And that also meant East Coker. In my case, the excitement was more specifically about offering my literary aspirations to the *Western Gazette*.

TWO

Hot Metal and Warm Bodies

I WAS DUE to start work at 7am on the following Monday. My mother got up to cut my sandwiches and sensibly implied that, because of bread rationing introduced the previous month, I'd do worse than buy fish and chips from Beswick's, just over the road from the newspaper office, once or twice later in the week. The prospect of regularly eating out like this filled me with embryonic notions of sophistication. I took especial care with my cycle clips, to protect my new suit.

'You're looking very smart, Matthew,' my mother said. My parents marked the day by standing at the front gate to wave me off. I cycled round the corner and up Tellis Hill, by now thoroughly self-conscious about my ostentatious brown pinstripe. To complete the ensemble, I was wearing a broadish-brimmed brown trilby. I'd noticed that most of the national paper reporters went in for trilbies. One of the Bristol evening papers also employed a young district man in Yeovil. I'd seen him come to cover my school's commemoration day speech. He appeared to take no notes at all and when he got up to leave, I was much impressed by his brown trilby. It was worn at a rakish angle and the brim, almost twice as wide as mine, was bent to make it even more pronounced. Graham was straight out of *The Front Page*; Hecht and MacArthur must have known him. Or perhaps he'd simply seen *The Front Page* too many times.

We were, in fact, to become firm if unlikely friends. I reverentially read his laconic news stories. He was tall, painfully thin and fearless when it came to upsetting self-important local government officials. He made no more than nominal appearances at council meetings but wrote whole columns of racy narrative about petty embezzlers, if they were well known and respected local figures, or wayward scout masters.

He was, I suppose, inclined to be a parody of a journalist – and it was the pithy parody I admired most of all. His preoccupation with American crime films rather bothered me. But our friendship was brief. In pseudo-Chandler style, he sent a memo to his news editor in Bristol. It said unequivocally: I QUIT. There was no other explanation. The following day he was seen loitering suspiciously in Oxford Street, London. He was found to have an automatic pistol and six rounds of ammunition on him. At Marlborough Street court he was fined £10, with the alternative of a month's imprisonment, for being in possession of the revolver without a firearms certificate.

But I am looking ahead too quickly. Heading for my first Monday morning of full employment, I passed only milk carts and newspaper boys. I reached the newspaper office by ten to seven and left my cycle in a narrow alley I found alongside the building. The *Gazette* building was one of sturdy, somewhat serious, appearance. It curved around from Sherborne Road into Newton Road and might have passed as a hospital.

The office was already ablaze with light. My trilby was obscured under my armpit as I climbed the five stone steps and went through the heavy wooden doors which were ajar. I hovered in the reception area, a stranger with neatly brushed-back hair, parted over the left eye, and double-breasted suit just out of the cutting room. Advertising clerks, as I was to conclude in the years that followed, were creatures consumed by curiosity. There were half a dozen of them in that front office, bespectacled and chirpy; they spied me and, as one, stopped opening the ever cascading mountain of mail, so that they could gaze at me through the glass partition. The roly-poly clerk nearest me eventually put down the ruler he was using to slit the envelopes and came to the hatch.

'Not open for business yet, old chap. Not till nine. What've you got – a death notice?'

Funny, I came to discover, the way death so often took precedence in the commercial well-being of the advertising department.

'Em-no. I've. . .I've come to start work today. As a copy boy.' It sounded, as I said it, slightly demeaning but that was what they'd called the job at my interview. 'Everyone begins as a copy boy, young Matthew,' they told me. So I imagined Ian Mackay and Noel Barber and Arthur Helliwell and Hannen Swaffer had. And that was good enough for me.

They pointed me up the stairs. 'Cherry'll look after you.' I heard some collective jollity from behind the glass.

'Cherry' Chapman was the assistant editor, the man who had interviewed me in a staid and quite paternal way. He hadn't been my idea of a newspaper dynamo. He was thin and pink-cheeked and always dressed, as I was to find out, in a suit of charcoal grey. His white collars were so stiff that his neck bore permanent red scars. He'd have passed for a deacon of the Free Church and I suspect a drop never passed his lips. Those lips had the curl of a constant smile, though you came to realise the expression was a fixture and registered no particular emotion.

I gingerly opened the door marked 'Sub-Editors' and immediately spotted him at the head of a long table, standing and peering through his glasses at a long, lean galley proof, in myopic anguish. The over-all atmosphere was that of a morgue. There were half a dozen subs of varying age, bulk and demeanour, spread around the table. They were bent over pieces of disfigured paper containing, it appeared, varying degrees of legibility, grammatical prowess and descriptive approximation to the meeting or match being covered. Most of the reports seemed to be handwritten. These six subs came in early on Monday and Thursday. Their doleful expressions implied that the arrangement didn't particularly please them.

I must be honest and admit that the corporate title of Sub-Editors much impressed me. These occupants had an elevated status, I assumed, only a minor degree or two removed from that of the editor himself. In the years that followed my initial impression was somewhat revised. 'You know what we do, son,' said one elder statesman of the office to me in the early days. 'We make sure the bloody words are spelt properly, we slash everything down to bloody size, and we put the bloody headlines on. What would you do without us?' I remember thinking at the time I should have replied with mordant delibera-tion: 'I just don't bloody know!' The sub-editors never went out of the office. They sat on their sore bottoms all day long and believed without exception that they could write better than the slandered reporters.

I began my hesitant walk towards the top of the table. My sensitive nostrils soon picked up the reek of stale beer as I passed one corner of the table. There were intermittent grunts of disgust and whole pages of laboriously handwritten prose were heaved onto the nearest spike – that practical, lethal-looking instrument on which misguided and rejected creativity was pierced and quartered before being gathered up periodically by the cleaners for the wastepaper baskets or stoke-hole. The long table was littered with unused and misused copy paper, daily papers, glue pots, scissors and miscellaneous reference props. There wasn't a single telephone but a built-in wooden cubicle housed one in the far corner of the room.

'Shit! I just can't take this effing bloke every week. Can't we pension the poor sod off?'

Rowly looked after sport. He was an embittered man who believed in sprinkling his profanities generously. He'd come back from the war and, as I was to discover, didn't find England any better than it was before. He regularly harangued no-one in particular on the state of the world, the hollow promises of the Labour government, a nation's ingratitude to Winston Churchill and buggers who stayed at home somehow missing the call-up while he and others went off to bust a gut to preserve our shores. Rowly had a spectacularly broken nose, generally understood to have been the result of a dislodged lavatory cistern during a bacchic frolic.

Cherry put down his fountain pen. His pink face twitched. 'I really must ask you to moderate your language.' Rowly only scowled and slammed another meandering report of a Perry Street League encounter on the spike.

As he looked up, the charcoal-grey-suited assistant editor saw me. 'Ah, yes, this is young Matthew. He's our new copy boy.' No-one took a blind bit of notice. 'Come on over here, alongside me. Gerald will show you what you've got to do.'

Gerald, or 'Buzz', was my predecessor, about the same age and now on the point of graduating to the reporters' room. He had been assigned to look after me for the first week. He had an engaging, cheeky manner and the prematurely lined, tubercular features of a young man who was either terminally ill or at least vastly hyperactive in the sexual sense.

My duties those early days weren't creatively taxing. I scurried up and down the stairs with messages that seemed to me of minimal importance, from and for the advertising department. Almost at once I detected the dividing line and intense rivalry between advertising and editorial. Snide remarks were constantly being traded. The apportioning of space each week could be a matter of open antagonism. I liked the advertising staff individually, especially the manager who hated unseemly fights and was apt to walk out of the office when an inter-departmental row was brewing. He kept goats and learned to play the church organ when he was sixty. Local advertisers liked him but he wasn't cut out for the more aggressive side of commerce. His front office workers were an arcane breed. They spent much of their day sitting on high stools, making entries in their ledgers with an artistic flourish. They also aped each other in eccentricities of speech. . . 'Ah, Mee-eester Fouracre. Have you another query from Mee-eester Chapman?' It was somewhere between pseudo-servile Dickensian and British B-pictures.

In addition, I felt I spent half my time in the composing room on the top floor, where the hot-metal machines rattled and clattered in a frenetic, unrelenting din. This was where I went to collect the galley proofs, singly or by the dozen. Occasionally I was sent outside the office – to buy cigarettes for the sub-editors.

On the third day the editor called me in. He was a small, intelligent man of unsmiling nature. He was well in with the Yeovil establishment: Rotary, the Civic Society and probably the Masons. He possessed an aura of authority, different from the kind I was experiencing in the subs' room. He clearly favoured gleaming black shoes and took a long, disconcerting look at my feet as he sized me down and up. The editor was in essence a Victorian. He ended our little chat by telling me that with the right degree of zeal I too could one day become a fine journalist like. . .'Mr Eynon, of Lymington. . .Mr House, of Blandford. . .Mr Whalley of Dorchester. . .and Mr Wyton here at head office.' I was relieved that he didn't go through the whole list of the *Gazette*'s district reporters. If he'd only said: '. . .like James Cameron and Harry Procter.'

In philanthropic tones that I found hard to equate with the offer on hand, he told me as a parting shot that I would be starting on twenty-five shillings a week. I should consider myself an apprentice learning my craft from experts.

As I left his office, I glanced around me. The room had a well-ordered, though dingy, ambience. He sat himself in a substantial leather chair, so high and upright that he was able to dangle his short legs three inches off the floor. The polished bookcases stocked what looked like drab, bulky reference works. I could pick out sporadic titles – about local government, the law, ecclesiastical matters. There were dozens of *Hansards*, neatly piled along one skirting. His desk itself surprised me. Three fountain pens were meticulously aligned alongside a virgin sheet of blotting paper. It might have been a bank manager's desk.

Cherry extended the benign lecture when I returned to the subs' room. 'I hope you have a reliable bicycle, young Matthew.' I nodded: 'A racer.'

'When your time comes to be a real reporter, you will be expected

25

to go round the country lanes for your paragraphs, just as I once did round the byways of Dorset. Some reporters, especially those on the evening papers, are given cars nowadays. It isn't the same. Pull up in a car outside a country cottage and you can frighten the life out of the old couple inside – they probably think it's the doctor or something. And a good resourceful reporter on a strong bicycle can get up lanes that are too narrow for cars. I know all about it, young Matthew. You can't beat a bike.' He liked the sound of that spontaneous slogan and paused for us both to appreciate it. As an afterthought, he said: 'Fuel is still very short in this country. We don't need petrol for a three-speed Raleigh, do we.' He actually laughed this time, as an appendage to the habitual smile.

It was a slack time of the day. Rowly, intellectually unfulfilled, was doing the *Telegraph* crossword. Blue smoke was corkscrewing from two pipes up towards the lofty ceiling. 'Clev', tall, introspective, kindly, had gone off to the lavatory for half an hour with the *Manchester Guardian*.

Cherry had spent the whole of his working life, after leaving school at fourteen, with the *Gazette*. He loved it, questioned nothing. He was a loyal, industrious weekly paper man. He couldn't make decisions but he'd earned the status of assistant editor for all the paragraphs of parochial mundaneness that he had posted to head office with unfailing enthusiasm, for all the muddy miles he'd clocked on his reliable three-speed.

Now, he considered, was a good moment to pursue his well-intentioned lecture. I looked at him, his wholesome, pink face, his pristine-white collar, and knew he should have been a lay preacher. Perhaps he was, I thought.

'I hope you're not like so many of the other young lads. Just wanting to move on to one of those dreadful evening papers, or worse. You can't do better than stay here – for a lifetime. We're a provincial paper. Nothing is too small, too insignificant. Do you realise, young Matthew, that the *Western Gazette* goes into almost every house in our five counties. Just think of that. What a responsibility that is! We give the readers what they expect. Nothing sensational, nothing too controversial. We've got the advertisers to think of – we've got the police and the local authorities to keep happy. It isn't our job to stir up trouble. People buy the *Gazette* because they know they can rely on it. It's their bible.'

So that was it. I was about to start writing the scriptures. But I found the enormity of the commitment, as outlined by the earnest assistant editor, difficult to reconcile with the paper's complementary prose – the smudgy Women's Institute reports and disjointed resumés of parish council meetings that came in voluminously by every post.

Both the strong language and the repressive air of gloom in the subs' room surprised me. It was a joy to go on my sorties into the composing room, where the linotype operators, with their pale faces and cunning twinkling eyes, perched on their machine seats and tapped away with the proficient rapidity of office typists, though the fingers were thick, gnarled and nicotine-stained. They would tease and shout their ribald jokes above the incessant chatter of the print equipment as lines of type were moulded in the hot metal.

I loved just to stand and watch; I was enthralled. I relished the smell of the place: the discernible tang of freshly rolled galley proofs, the ink still glistening and wet, the whiff of menthol snuff and, at stipulated times, of strong shag tobacco.

As another alternative to the oppressive severity of the sub-editors' room, there was, again on the upper floor, the reading room. This was where the proofs were read against the original copy by a team of girls, supervised by the head reader, a tall, beaky and forbidding individual. The girls read aloud at great speed, in an acquired high-pitched sing-song voice. To the eavesdropper, they sang foreign incantations with a puzzling south Somerset accent.

The warm aroma of young female bodies, of heavy-handed make-up and perfume, lent allure and sensuality to the top floor. Whenever I was sent in with a query I blushed. The girls treated me as a diversion to the eye-straining ritual of a thousand auction sale notices that had to be meticulously checked. They'd look up and give me a cupid-lipped grin. One or two of them were noticeably nubile and I was soon making excuses to return with nebulous queries – to the irritation of the head reader, who adhered to the apparent non-Conformist characteristics of the various heads of department. The girls would clatter down the stairs in their platform shoes at lunchtime. They were always gossiping, often it seemed to me in the same high-pitched vocal style their job demanded. The cheap scent lingered on the stairs long after they'd gone. It was very much to my liking.

As the week went on, I gained enough confidence to shuffle into the reporters' room, next door. It was small, oddly shaped in a sheepish semi-circle. A frayed carpet covered part of the floor. There were three little tables and as many antique-piece Underwood typewriters. The room had no other furniture and no telephone.

The occupants were a far more approachable lot. Stuart was the chief reporter. He'd been taken on the staff in the late Thirties on the strength of an article he had daringly submitted and had printed by the *Daily Mail*, criticising his grammar school's attitude to homework. Now he was another bloke back from the war, during which he'd served for a long time in the desert and risen to the unlikely rank of sergeant major. Don was short, ebullient and had Goonish features halfway between Secombe and Bentine. Someone may have told him of the resemblance; he developed a nervous, manic laugh. Mary was a warm-hearted Scot whose peerless Pitman's kept the department going while the majority of her colleagues had been collared to do their bit. She was Calvinistic and, although she would never have complained, no-one swore in her presence.

Nowadays her duties were more secretarial. She possessed a most generous nature and was much put upon because of it. There was a single decent, modern typewriter on the whole of that floor, shared by all for the really important letters. Mary had borrowed it and was humping the excessively heavy machine from one room to the next after typing a letter for the editor, when I clumsily threw open the reporters' door. The typewriter was knocked from her hands and clattered to the floor. Yards of ribbon spilled out, screws were loosened and keys became intertwined. Flustered and inarticulately apologetic, I picked the bruised machine up and placed it on a table. Mary had a technical bent, unlike me. Gradually, patiently she righted the typewriter's internal injuries. She never got away from work on time and my ham-fisted entry must have irritated her immensely. She had saintly qualities and said only: 'Never mind, we'll see what we can do.'

The reporters went in for Fair Isle sweaters and sports coats, the pockets of which were always bulging with at least three thick notebooks. Most of them seemed to smoke a good deal and, ever impressionable, I was soon digging into my twenty-five shillings gross for a packet of Woodbines, the cheap, strong, proletarian brand favoured by my father. By my standards, the reporters were also a worldly bunch. Several of them were engaged in hushed conversation one late afternoon as I peeped in. 'Buzz' was the centre of their attention. He had two small containers of ointment in his hands.

They looked at each other and then flatteringly decided I was ready for matters of confidentiality. 'Buzz thinks he may have caught a dose!'

I took it in the best traditions of British phlegm. Buzz was looking more pallid than usual. But he had a resilient sense of murky humour.

28

He might only just have ended his spell as copy boy yet he savoured a captive audience. He wasn't averse to a bit of autobiographical narrative. And he went on to give us all a graphic account of his visit earlier that day to the surgery of an Austrian-Jewish doctor in the town. 'He said to me, "Down wiz ze trousers, zen," and gave me a good going-over. He asked me what I'd been doing with my spare evenings and then gave me this muck to smear on the offending section of the genitals.'

Buzz was a great reader of D.H. Lawrence and any other avant-garde literature, as we saw it then, which dealt with strong sexual themes. His phraseology on the subject could be oddly formal and sophisticated. I'd hardly heard anyone talk of genitals before. 'The doc isn't sure. May not be anything serious at all.'

The rest of us in the room privately pledged not to use the communal lavatory seat in a cavalier fashion for a few weeks. We plumped for safety.

My new found friends in the reporters' room maintained a consciously elevated position, all the same, in their relationship with me. I was just the copy boy and there had to be a defined order of status within the office. It took them some weeks before they invited me to share a half at the Elephant across the road. They bragged with superior glee, in my hearing, of what they had heard as evidence in the domestic courts – 'Can't use a bloody line of that but it's great stuff' – and of chummy exchanges with the 'Super' on the morning police calls. They enjoyed using new words and vied in the efforts to extend the room's vocabulary. To my surprise, they played Hang the Man as they killed time before their next assignments. They went in for unlikely words, 'Syphilitic' stumped them on the first day I looked in on the contest. Maybe it was understandable that there was such a current preoccupation with the subject.

The *Western Gazette* came out on Friday; so Thursday was the 'press day'. The character of the building then changed. There was much rushing around and needless extremes of urgency. Over-cautious subs kept re-reading proofs, losing faith in their earlier judgment and taking out whole paragraphs. By first thing on Thursday the page plans had taken shape, although often they had been virtually predetermined by late Tuesday, irrespective of news value. Page make-up seldom changed, whatever the variations of content through the thirteen editions. The type was bedded straight up and down, with turns into the next column where necessary. Most of the stories were single-column. There was no question of saving the best of them for the front page. Advertisements still took up the whole of the front. It was a grey, monotonous slab of small type, dominated by the auctioneers and chartered surveyors, with news of their coming sales. Senior & Godwin, Jackson Stops & Staff, Cooper & Tanner, Palmer & Snell. . .they sounded more like music-hall acts to me.

It was mid-morning on the Thursday that I saw Cherry and one of the other subs deep in perplexed conversation. They were scrutinising a sheet of paper, alternating whispered suggestions with long silences.

Eventually Cherry came across to me. 'Matthew,' he said, with dramatic deliberation, 'I'm going to give you your first important job.' Then he ascertained that I'd brought my cycle with me.

He handed me the sheet of paper which turned out to be a wedding form of the kind the *Gazette* sent to all prospective married couples. The basic questions were printed and the bride-to-be or her mother was expected to fill in the details. The assistant editor was shaking his head as if he were ruminating on grave, maybe even libellous, errors. He gave me a look of prodigious professional challenge. 'Have you ever been to Stoke-under-Ham?' I nodded; of course, I had. Paris, Rome and Athens, maybe not yet. Stoke-under-Ham, yes.

In moments of crisis, 'important' was Cherry's favourite word. 'A quite important family, these people. I'm practically certain the bride's father is on the parochial church council. But do you know what they've done – they've forgotten to describe the bride's wedding dress. It's important. The readers like to know, young Matthew. We've been trying to get them on the phone but it's out of order. We could leave the report over to next week but by then it would be nearly three weeks old.'

He gave me another of his challenging stares. 'I want you to cycle out and see the family. Take the form with you and fill in the missing details. Give the family our compliments.'

Again he made me aware of my new professional stature. 'Time's against us, my lad. It may be the last edition to go but I shall need you back here by early afternoon. Remember that it's still got to be written up, and then set. I'm relying on you.'

It might have been Coward, heavy with gold braid, saying that last sentence to young rating Attenborough.

I was grateful for the errand which took me out of the office. I got to Stoke, nestling under Ham Hill, and found the family in just over half an hour. Studiously – and, dare I say, importantly – I made a longhand note of the bride's nuptial splendour. On the way home, realistically unmindful of my assistant editor's paranoia over the time factor, I parked my cycle against the side of the pavement outside the Phelips Arms at Montacute and ordered half a pint of home-brewed. It was my subconscious statement that I had grown up, ready to break the journey with an ale. The pub also had romantic connotations for me: I had read it was where the brilliant, unschooled poet and hymnsmith, Thomas Shoel, had sat on a beer barrel in the eighteenth century to create spontaneously his musical notes for a brass band who'd arrived with their instruments.

It still wasn't even 1.30 when I got back and climbed the stairs of the *Gazette*. Cherry was waiting. 'Got it for you, Mr Chapman.'

'Good lad, Matthew.' Again the fixed smile which always made me want to smile back in acknowledgement. 'Now I'm going to see what you can do. Tell me, do you think you can take this completed wedding form and write it up and – ' He suddenly broke off. 'Have you been drinking?'

I had already been forewarned that a penetrative question like this from the abstemious Mr Chapman was guaranteed to damn the victim with all the guilt of a philanderer caught in coital midstream by a returning husband.

I mumbled that I had snatched a five-minute liquid lunch so that I'd be ready to start on any writing that needed doing. He wasn't convinced. 'That foul stuff will do you no good at all. In our job we need to keep our head clear – and our breath sweet. I can tell you that the best reporters on the *Western Gazette* don't bother themselves with strong drink.' It wasn't what I'd been told.

As I assumed a suitably contrite expression, Cherry returned to more immediate journalistic matters. 'I shall expect three nicely written paragraphs. Stick to the facts, nothing else. We like to start with "The wedding took place". Or, occasionally for rather special ceremonies, "The marriage was solemnised". We don't depart from that.' He studied the form again, eyes six inches from the sheet. 'You can include that touches were rung on the parish bells and the honeymoon was spent at Weston-super-Mare. Remember the hyphens there. And whatever you do, spell the names right. Now then, go over there and sit down. I want you to do it in your best handwriting. No need to be typed. But the compositors must be able to read it.'

Yes, sir. Thank you, sir. Can I have my geometry book back, sir. Dear old, well intentioned Cherry had made me feel that I was back at school. But I wasn't – I was about to churn out my first piece for the *Gazette*. I took a pile of muddy-white copy paper and began to write. I knew all about catchlines and nonchalantly wrote 'Wedding 1' at the top right-hand corner. Then I started. 'The wedding took place. . .'

On the Friday morning, the *Gazette* hadn't arrived by the time I left home, though I had hovered for an extra ten minutes in the hope that I might see the paper boy. At the office the atmosphere was noticeably relaxed. Cherry was standing, spreading a copy of the paper in front of him in a pose of patent self-congratulation.

It was a slack day for me. There was scope for me to sit at my little side table and go through the Yeovil edition with almost academic interest. I read the town 'pars' which tumbled into the paper in a steepling column: the Gay Nineties Club, Weekend Services at the Salvation Army Temple, Fabian Society, Adult School, Meeting of Mesopotamian War Veterans and, over the column at my beloved East Coker, seven succinct lines that listed the Beetle Drive Prize-winners.

My rapacious eye moved on; there were more significant pearls to find. There were just eight crowded pages, all that was allowed because of the newsprint shortage, and I found the wedding report at the third attempt, fighting a losing battle for recognition between all the stifling columns of small ads. 'Touches on the parish bells' was the heading.

I'd given them three paragraphs, spot on, as ordered. In the third par, I read knowingly that the bride wore a dress of white and duck-egg blue and had burgundy accessories. The reception was held at the Cottage Café, another stunning addition I had gleaned from the family. I checked the spelling of the names and they were correct. Surreptitiously, I cut out the report and put it in my breast pocket.

It was, I decided, a pretty good report. And, well, more or less all my own work.

Cherry picked up his rolled umbrella; he was about to take the rest of the day off. 'If things are quiet, you should be able to leave early this afternoon. Maybe we'll find another wedding report for you next week.' He had moved quite close to me and I suspected he was probably checking my breath for remnants of the night before. Did he really think that callow sixteen-year-olds on twenty-five bob a week had the same alcoholic capacity as embittered, unfulfilled Rowly?

Buzz showed me how to log all the district reporters' engagements for the coming week. I filed the thirteen editions for the current issue.

I pulled out from my pocket and read sadly the various obituaries I'd cut from the national papers the previous day of my boxing idol, flyweight Benny Lynch, the Glaswegian lush.

By three o'clock the subs' room was sepulchral-still. Clev was alone, puffing at his pipe and reading the *New Statesman*. The reporters' room was deserted. Did nothing happen on a Friday in Yeovil or the surrounding villages, I asked myself? Clev suggested it was time for me to go, too.

I left my cycle in the *Gazette* yard and walked up the hill to the Central Cinema, which I liked more for its art deco style of architecture than its stuffy interior. I was humming Donald Peers' 'Babbling Brook'. Yeovil School was already a long way away. I snuggled down with Margaret Lockwood, enunciating beautifully in *Dear Octopus*.

A lot had happened in a week. A lot of proofs, a lot of new faces. And a wedding report all my own. By now I'd discarded my new brown suit, to save it from printer's ink stains and mocking glances. I was back to a sports coat.

THREE

Libel

CHERRY WAS a creature of habit. Whenever a message was relayed to him or a phrase in one of the more reputable papers took his fancy, he committed it to his notebook. He recorded it in flawless shorthand, using the kind of expensive fountain pen which had been given him, I imagined, by fellow church stewards as a fiftieth birthday present. I rarely saw him write anything in longhand, apart from his signature at the foot of an official letter – a letter which contained many of the identical clichés and cumbersome constructions that monopolised the *Gazette's* conservative and stylised columns.

One day he caught me looking over his shoulder at his picturesque Pitman's. 'I hope one day, young man, you will have a note as neat as mine. It's the greatest asset one of our journalists can possess – reliable shorthand.'

Bang went my preconceived notions that creative imagination and intrepid prying were the priceless virtues of my trade.

'We have arranged for you to go to Mrs Perkins' for lessons. She will make you highly proficient in six months. Young Gerald is already coming along nicely. All of our head office reporters have reason to be grateful to Mrs Perkins, you know. . .We shall pay for your lessons.'

There was no end to the generosity, though frankly I'd have preferred another five bob in my pay packet.

My opening lesson was on the following Monday. It was quite a revelation: a bizarre example of intensive small-town commercial tuition. There were seven of us, mostly pudding-faced and inanimate typists, seated around the small table, in a poky, badly lit living room. The curtains were heavy and oppressive. The room had a stuffy, faded Edwardian look to it. I'm not sure if there was an aspidistra but there should have been.

Mrs Perkins herself was rather glum and menopausal, and at the same time touchingly child-like. She talked to us in a way a mother would to a five-year-old. This tone was extended to two smelly, over-fed ginger cats that vied for our chairs, occasionally got onto the table and eternally brushed against our feet, to add to the acute claustrophobia. Maybe the reason Mrs Perkins was a successful teacher of shorthand was because we were always doing our best to complete the course and wave an eager goodbye to the ginger toms that dominated the living room and her thoughts.

She was a heavy breasted woman and her fulsome torso rested awkwardly on the tablecloth as she leaned across to correct one of our tentative hieroglyphics. 'We must keep at it, mustn't we. Then one day, it will be as easy as driving a car,' she trilled. It was, I remember thinking at the time, very unlikely that she'd ever driven a car.

I kept my shorthand book at my side back in the office and my pink-cheeked mentor appeared to approve of my conscientious regard for professional betterment. At the same time, I pledged privately never to become a slave to it – I saw senior reporters coming back from council meetings with endless pages of Pitman's. Salient points, I felt, must surely get buried in the sheer volume of meaningless, self-indulgent words.

There was still, after all, little space to spare in the paper. A letter which the *Gazette* printed summed it up:

> I am very concerned that although the *Western Gazette* cannot accept subscriptions because of the restrictions on the supply of paper, a football pools firm can send me four enclosures offering to forward me coupons every week. What an extraordinary situation – you are debarred from freely selling your newspaper and I am debarred from obtaining information. And yet at the same time, the directors of a football pool apparently have so much paper available that they are in a position to scatter unsolicited literature to all parts of the country. . .

In fact, a few weeks later, the Government announced that more newsprint would be made available. The size of the *Gazette* was going up from eight to ten pages.

Buzz remained my confidant. We both agreed Cherry had our interest at heart, though he was too damned paternalistic for our liking. 'He's away seeing some of his district men on Wednesday – you've got to make the most of it,' said my companion. He was in a particularly breezy mood, influenced by encouraging news from his Austrian-Jewish quack.

By felicitous coincidence, Clev asked me on the Wednesday to buy some tobacco for him, an obscure brand which was only sold at a shop at the other end of the town. 'Great,' said Buzz when he heard, 'just right for the Cadena.'

Over the next few years, morning coffee at the Cadena was to become a joy for me, not for the quality of the beans or the relatively genteel ambience of the restaurant – but because this was always the meeting point for up to half a dozen local reporters, working for the weekly and evening papers. It often meant for me a brisk, guilt-ridden walk up Middle Street followed by a frantic sprint down again. But I came to love the ritual: the hilarity and the gossip, everything so unstuffy. Current news stories were debated and laughed about. We sat apart from the more conventional elements of Yeovil's morning-coffee society.

On my Cadena debut, Buzz introduced me to several journalists I didn't yet know, including 'Sib', an amiable evening paper veteran who had both an extravagant bow tie and double chin. I was referred to as the newest member of the *Gazette's* editorial staff, not a copy boy. There's honour and tact among colleagues at the lower end of the scale.

The restaurant had in those days three pretty young waitresses. One of them had pouty lips and the worldly, predatory ways of perhaps a twenty-two-year-old who'd already been married, was near to divorce and on the point of relaunch in pursuit of prey. That, as I discovered later, was precisely her state of life. She wore slippers and glided round the first-floor tables as if in a bedroom. She could balance the cups on the tray exquisitely. Her eyes were full of nuances. I was caught peeping. 'Seen her, have you? Knows what it's for, doesn't she? We're all a bit scared of her,' one of the older reporters said with a knowing wink.

Her marital status and doubtless extra-marital experiences gave her the edge on her fellow waitresses. She was conscious of her sensuality. It wasn't that she flaunted it but, as she lowered the coffee cups onto the table with languid deliberation, she gave me improper feelings I'd never fully known before.

She had a husky voice, less West Country than the other girls. 'Which paper are you on, then?' she asked me.

The bubbling conversation on the table was instantly stilled. My face burned. 'The *Gazette*.'

'I didn't think I'd seen you before.' The dialogue was brief and mundane. To me it was quite bewitching.

When she glided away, hips swaying, the good-natured mocking started. 'You've got a chance there, Matt.' 'She's sniffed out a new face. Watch yourself, old son.' I wriggled happily in my seat. I knew they were teasing me but, aroused by the kind of powerful, private emotions that we all savoured at that age, I didn't mind at all.

Fearful that Clev would think I was altogether too long buying his tobacco, I realised I had to leave before the others. I got up and asked haltingly: 'Where do we pay?' I was told with an undisguised leer: 'Pick up the bill from Diana as you go out.'

The prospect made me blush again and I hoped no-one noticed. I waved a gauche goodbye to my new-found friends and hovered clumsily as Diana served another table. She saw me and smiled. 'You haven't given me the bill yet – how much please?' I asked with uneasy formality.

She lifted up her little pad, fixed to a cord around her waist. Something was scribbled and then, very deliberately, she screwed up the minute invoice. 'That's it then – em?' 'Matthew. I'm called Matthew. But I've not – '

'You've paid. . . see you again one day.' And she was gone in those bedroom slippers, swaying from the lips as well as the hips.

I walked down the stairs, already in love for the first time with a twenty-two-year-old divorcee who was disconcertingly sexy and didn't charge me sixpence for my coffee. On the walk of untold elation back to the office, I went over our duologue a dozen times. It was better, more loaded, than any of the intimate exchanges I'd seen in *Casablanca* only the other day.

The drudgery of proof-collecting, and occasionally proof-pulling when the more militant members of the union weren't looking, continued. I came to know every linotype operator, every stone-hand. . . and most members of the reading room, in my shy way, by their Christian name. At ten to two, when the reporters weren't around, I'd go into their office and look out of the window by standing on the hot-water pipes. That gave me a good view of the road – and the first sight of the girls as they returned after lunch. There was also, at this time of the day, much activity in the doorway of the newsagent's across the road. It had to do, I came to learn, with the taking of illegal bets.

On one Thursday morning, I was told there was a job which would take me out of the building. I was to go to the magistrates' court and collect copy from one of our senior reporters there. Several 'important' cases were in process and because this was edition-day,

the reports had to be written up on the spot and rushed back for sub-
bing and setting. Something which was to become commonplace for
me and many others was in those distant days a matter of twitching
apprehension. 'It's not easy, young Matthew. But we all have to do
it at some time. That's why a good shorthand note is so vital. You
can't afford to make a mistake with a court case.'

I was given military-like instructions on how to tiptoe my way
into the courtroom and sit, in deferential silence, alongside our man
in the press box. It was an exciting commitment for me. I'd never
been inside a magistrates' court before.

The court door squeaked as I gingerly pushed it open. Everyone
turned; it was quite awful. But I recognised our man and moved in
next to him. The solicitor, momentarily interrupted, picked up his
threads again. 'So you see, your worships, this is really in effect a
technical offence, nothing more. . . an innocuous contravention of
the emergency powers forced on us by the shortages that come with
our – er – postwar austerities.'

Our man drew closer to me and whispered: 'I've written up the main
case from the special Juvenile Court this morning. And now this one
is nearly over. You can hang on and take both of them back.'

I glanced around the panelled and sombre setting. Then I bit my
lip, partly in sympathy, as I saw the middle-aged man in the dock.
I'd never seen a defendant this close to sentence before. His face
was strained and I wondered what dastardly crime he'd committed.
Larceny? Assault? Forgery? Murder, even. . .? To my disappointment, there were no men in wigs. The magistrates looked glum and
forbidding.

The juvenile case was pushed over to me. It was written in pencil
and ran to nine folios. There were many abbreviations. Yeovil was
'Yvl', that was 'tt' and so on. Whole strings of words were joined
up and I wondered however the compositors translated. And as the
solicitor, a pompous man I had previously seen as one of my school
governors, droned on in what turned out to be his closing speech for
the defence, I read the proficiently scribbled report in front of me.

Two children had played truant from school and had stolen a live
chicken from the station master at Pen Mill. The parents had been
in tears and one of the boys hadn't been able, according to the police
officer, to write his name on the statement; he'd put a mark instead.
I shuddered to myself at this commentary on postwar education.

I knew the station master, a pleasant little man called Len who
sang in the local operatic society and wouldn't from my experience

have wanted to make a serious issue out of the loss of one of his Rhode Island Reds which every day diced with death as a convoy of noisy and lethal locos clattered past their embankment homestead. It pleased me to read on the third page of the case: 'Mr Hole, the station master, was loath to prosecute, your worships, and reduced the value of the chicken from twelve shillings to six shillings in an attempt to mitigate the offence. . .'

The last paragraph went: 'After a short retirement, it was decided that the case against the two boys should be dismissed.' I thought of the weeping mothers and made one of my normal, emotional judgments. Justice had been done.

By this time the closing speech had been finished and the five magistrates had shuffled out for their deliberations and a smoke. Our man was writing away, showing off slightly and passing me the sheets of completed copy one after the other.

The opening par left a blank where the fine had to be inserted when the magistrates returned. I was much impressed by the journalistic technique – and the sense of edition-day urgency. So the staid, ever reliable old *Gazette* really could step on the gas when necessary.

As handed to me, the report read:

Alfred John Crowther, of the Mermaid Hotel, Yeovil was fined. . . at Yeovil Magistrates' Court yesterday for contravention of the Meals in Establishment Order 1946, by supplying with a main meal bread which did not constitute an integral part of a dish containing other food – nor was it supplied to a person who specifically asked for it.

That was the first paragraph and I felt there were better ways of writing English. I wasn't quite sure what it meant. But I also accepted that the reporter couldn't depart too far from the jargon of the charge-sheet. I read on:

For the prosecution, it was stated that Mr William Webber, an enforcement officer to the Ministry of Food, had lunch at the Mermaid Hotel. There were other people seated at the table, on which was a plate of rolls and bread. The defendant came up to the table with small slices of bread which he offered to Mr Webber, who refused them.

The defence claimed that bread had been left there from breakfast and was going stale. Mr Crowther thought it preferable to offer it to the hotel guests than give it to the pigs. He could after all have covered the bread with gravy and served it, without commiting any offence.

As if to show that the hotel had the nation and its shortages in mind, the defence continued, it should be recorded that the Mermaid had cut its weekly bread bill from £1 10s to 15s 9d.

The magistrates came back and I scrambled to my feet, following the example of everyone else. They were looking both self-righteous and self-conscious. Their fine was a nomimal one of five shillings and I approved of the way it seemed to carry an implicit dislike for the way the prosecution had been brought. Bread rationing had been introduced in the July of 1946 and in the Brown Windsor soup days that followed, it was made very clear to us when we had our statutory five-shilling meal that bread was one of the dishes, never an extra. It was a temporary law of the land and not a very practical one. Better for pigs, than humans, I concluded.

I hurried back to the office, clutching my two batches of copy paper. My mind was on the second case. Did the Ministry of Food really go in for that kind of sneaky behaviour, I asked myself?

The subs studied the two handwritten reports. There was some stroking of chins. The reference to tears from the parents in the juvenile case was summarily struck out by Cherry's expensive fountain pen. He never considered it was the role of the reporter to relay such displays of emotion. 'Just stick to the facts,' he'd say repeatedly, as if it wasn't a fact that a distressed mother was moved to tears.

Passages from the Mermaid Hotel case were read aloud to the other sub-editors. Rowly, who used to drink there when not at the Duke of York next door to his home, sympathised with the manager. 'Those buggers from the Ministry. . . nothing better to do. . . worse than the bloody Gestapo. . .'

By now, after several weeks at the *Gazette*, my creative frustrations were growing. They led me to type what, for a callow copy boy, was a quite intrepid memo to the editor. It said: 'I think it is dreadful the way the Ministry of Food sneakily brought a case against a local hotel the other day. I am sure many of our readers feel the same way. Might it be a good idea to find out how many of these prosecutions have come to court – and the methods used? Would you allow me, in my spare time, to write a short feature on the subject. I think it would be worth talking to one of those enforcement officers.' As a postscript, I added: 'If there is no space for a proper feature, perhaps you would let me write a letter for publication in the paper.'

My memo brought a very prompt reply. The editor called me in. He seemed rather irritated; he didn't ask me to sit down as far as I remember. 'Now, young man, I don't want you to think that I disapprove of honest initiative. But I'm afraid you are being very naive. You should know, for a start, that it isn't our policy for members of staff to find their way into the correspondence column.

That space is made available for our readers – for leading councillors, civic officials, Members of Parliament, who have matters they need to raise. . .'

He looked again at my missive. 'I don't think your idea for a feature is a very good or wise one, do you? We like to remain impartial, not start criticising emergency laws of the land. The enforcement officer was merely making sure the rules weren't being broken.'

That was it. He'd either missed the point of my audacious memo or, more likely, had no intention of letting a copy boy loose on sensitive Ministry territory. The editor's phone rang, saving us from any more pointless conversation. He waved me to the door, saying as I turned, with a kindlier tenor to his voice: 'Your chance will come one day. But we must find the right subject to write about, mustn't we. . . Maybe we can arrange with Mr Chapman for you to come along with us to Rotary Club next Tuesday. Would you like that?'

'Yes, please,' I lied. I walked out even more frustrated and wondering whether Yeovil's good Rotarians had bread as an extra.

For the time being, none of the reporters showed any inclination to leave for more lucrative and rewarding pastures. That left me with my galley proofs, when not addressing the district men's envelopes and fetching Clev's tobacco as alternatives to the restricting office routine.

In those days, linage – the practice of reporters writing surreptitiously for other papers – was considered from on high at the *Gazette* as a heinous crime. Most of the editorial staff did it in varying degrees; one or two of the subs weren't averse to some stealthy 'milking' of copy. 'I don't want ever to hear of you writing stories for those dreadful evening papers,' Cherry had said at our first interview. I soon discovered, of course, it was a realistic way of supplementing a meagre pay-slip. It also gave scope for a hint or two of individuality and imagination.

Graham, he of the transatlantic accent, rakish trilby and penchant for crime movies, sensed my mounting frustrations. He let me write a short weekly column for his paper's Saturday Pink 'Un. I was even allowed, anonymously, to opinionate about the local football club. Just three hundred words – and seven and sixpence. I was always waiting for the Pink 'Un when it arrived down from Bristol at half past six. I read my little column at least three times: not from conceit but because, in effect, it was my sum total of weekly journalism.

I knew that some of the senior reporters were sending pieces to the national papers. It was a cloak-and-dagger operation. They would say to me, from the safety of the insulated office of theirs: 'See that story about the Bradford Abbas bigamy in the *Express*? That was mine, you know.' The pride and prestige were undeniable.

My chance came one Thursday afternoon as I sat at my side table practising my Pitman's. Wilf, a breezy clerk from the managing director's room downstairs, came in and chortled: 'Mr Chapman, there's some scruffy bloke at the counter. Says he's got a story. Works for the council, on the roads up in Goldcroft. Can someone go down. But don't be too long – he's probably got his drill and shovel outside.'

Counter callers, in search of publicity or in anger at transposed initials in flower-show reports, were frequent. They were often bumptious. The tales they told could be fatuous and time-wasting. Some were vagrants or quarrelsome drunks heaved out of the Elephant at closing-time. The front counter was also a popular haven for the unbalanced. The 'resurrected Christ' looked in once a month; his text was tenuous and interminable, and he was reluctant to leave. When the summons came, the rule was for the least active reporter to be sent down to see what it was all about. This Tuesday there was no reporter at all to be found. Buzz was missing, perhaps discreetly seeking additional medical reassurance.

Cherry looked round the subs' room. Heads were down. Sub-editors never considered it was part of their job to become office boys again and make polite conversation with madcap intruders, not fobbed off by the advertising staff who were in the best position to make the first judgment.

'Just go down to the counter, young Matthew. Someone wants a word with us. He may be rude. He may be unreasonable. He may be – em – a little scruffy. But he may still have information for us. See what he wants. Make no promises. And come back and ask, if you're in any doubt at all.' I was given the kind of look which suggested I was very much a last resort as the editorial ambassador to see a corporation roadman.

I went down and the man at the counter did actually have a shovel still in his hand. 'You a reporter, then?'

It was no moment for sheepish modesty. I nodded, producing a virgin reporter's notebook to back up my credentials. 'Got summik fer you. But do 'ee pay fer tip offs?'

Scruffy he may have been – but here, I concluded, was a resourceful council worker who'd maybe done this kind of thing before. I suspected that the *Gazette* left such pecuniary practices in the name of provincial journalism to the accursed evening papers. 'Er – I don't think so.'

'Pity, that, I might have to gi' it to summun else – *Post* or the *World*. They gi' half a crown for a good tip, you know.' I said cautiously that I'd take his name and address and check on editorial policy after I'd heard what the story was about.

It was a good one, all right. He'd been repairing a pavement outside a house, when he eavesdropped on the domestic conversation. A couple in their early seventies were due to get married. They had been sweethearts after leaving school. Then they went their separate ways and each married. The man went to live in the States and eventually lost his wife. His original sweetheart, back in Somerset, lost her husband. She went off to America, was persuaded to get in touch with her first love again. . . and that was it. My informant with the shovel was strong on narrative. 'Bloody good yarn, don't 'ee agree?' I did. I took the number of the house – and promised my source that I'd be writing to him if any half-crowns could be conjured up. But I implied that I wasn't too hopeful.

To be honest, I gained the impression that he should have been working for us full time instead of mending pavements. He had all the instincts of a news reporter. I wondered whether he spent all his time listening to private conversations and then relaying them for modest gain. I assumed a voice steeped in canny newspaper experience and said as he left the office: 'Don't hesitate to call in again.'

On the way up the stairs, my imagination was hurtling ahead. This one, this story, was going to be all mine.

'And what was that all about?' asked Mr Chapman as if he'd been waiting all the time with extreme anxiety for my return.

I affected minimal interest. 'Someone called in to tell us about a wedding taking place next week. Up at Goldcroft. Shall I cycle up with a form on my way home?'

It was agreed that I should. Dear old Cherry appeared so patently relieved that I hadn't been down at the counter offering presumptuous wisdom on behalf of the *Gazette* to anyone as important as maybe a soroptimist president, rural dean or, perish the thought, a grandmaster from the editor's lodge.

That evening I arrived at the house. On an early page of my notebook, I had thoughtfully tabulated eight or nine questions, to bolster my confidence. I propped my bike against a lamp-post and stalled, rather nervously, as I took off my cycle clips. Then I knocked at the door.

An elderly, glum-looking man with a crew cut and an incongruously cheerful tie opened it. I said I was from the *Gazette* and understood he was about to get married. Would he let me write about it? He was taken by surprise, suspicious about the way we had learned about the reunion. 'Oh, I think it was someone in the office. These things get around – you can't keep them all to yourself, you know.'

The suspicious, crew-cropped Mr Ricketts led me hesitantly in to meet his wife-to-be. She looked even glummer, an expression that was intensified when it was explained that I wanted to write about the approaching nuptials. 'Doris here, you must understand, doesn't like publicity. Neither do I. But, well Doris, what do you think? They'd do it quite nicely in the *Gazette*, I daresay. Nice and dignified. Nothing that we could take exception to.'

There were religious tracts, tastefully framed, on all the walls. Marriage for two staid septuagenarians could be an embarrassing business. Deadly dull, too, it seemed to me, when there should have been so much joy.

I sat at the table and asked my eight or nine questions. Studiously, I took down the answers in longhand. Those answers came slowly and reluctantly, and that helped my note-taking. 'We'd rather have nothing at all. Nothing. Not at our age. We don't go in for all that fuss and nonsense,' Doris kept repeating. I nodded with insincere sympathy. 'Don't worry, there'll be nothing to be embarrassed about. Just a few lines to have as a record – to please your friends.' I shook hands, congratulated the gloomy couple and cycled home with my first real story in my pocket.

There was egg-in-nest, poached egg encircled by mashed potato, for tea, a wartime nosset sustained by my mother because of its domestic popularity. Then I went to my new typewriter, bought for £3 19s 6d. The story wrote itself, even for a boy freshly out of school. It began: 'Nearly half a century ago, two teenage Yeovil sweethearts parted company. . .' The story ran for nine lengthy *Gazette*-style paragraphs. I worked in the answers to all my carefully framed questions. The report was a good deal longer than Mr and Mrs Ricketts would have wished.

Next morning I presented it on Mr Chapman's desk. 'I checked on that wedding up in Goldcroft last night. It turned out a bit unusual. I hope you don't mind, Mr Chapman, I've written it up myself.'

My nine paragraphs were read quickly, slowly and then a third time. Cherry read them with his glasses on and his glasses off. He pursed his lips; twice he gazed at me in a vague, abstract way with those smiling lips that weren't smiling. Before he offered any kind of reaction, he passed the sheets of copy paper to his nearest colleague. 'What do you think, Clev? Young Matthew here has handed it in. Done it off his own bat when all the facts could have gone on a wedding form. How safe is it?'

Safe? I couldn't follow. Clev made a far quicker judgment. 'Good story. . . yes, a good story, that. Well done, son.' The praise prompted Mr Chapman to add his muted congratulations, followed by a searing inquisition about the accuracy of my facts. Had I spelt the names right? Was I sure about their ages. . . and, oh yes, we never gave a woman's age. . . and how reliable could I possibly be without shorthand?

By mid-morning, after yet another inspection of my fledgling prose, this time by the editor, the report disappeared from view altogether. To my surprise and joy late in the afternoon, as I went to the composing room in search of a proof of the coming week's leader, I spied my story. Already set, too: a single-column piece that was almost a foot long, with hardly a phrase of mine taken out. The proof had been freshly pulled and was prominently spiked on a crooked nail along with the rest of the early South Somerset copy. 'Romance Began at Yeovil' was the headline. The instructions at the top of the proof were unequivocal: 'Precede Yeovil'. That meant the story was destined for one of the most prized positions in the paper – immediately before the avidly read town paragraphs.

'My story, Ron,' I said to the man who had just pulled the proof. It was no time to be modest. 'Like an extra one, would you?' he asked. I was schoolboyishly eager in nodding. His hairy, tattooed arms were smudged with printer's ink. I can still remember him handing me my story.

In the sheer romance of my prentice journalism, I kept recalling the precise phrasing of my piece as I lay in bed that night. I knew it was a good tale and I should have liked to give it a slightly less turgid treatment – though at the same time thrilled to have been given so much space. Intuition told me my story would be lifted by one of my older colleagues and sent to a Sunday paper. Why not get in first? The thought of such a challenge made me tingle.

Before I went to work next morning, I typed four crisp paragraphs about the Ricketts' reunion. At the top of the folio, I wrote: 'Matthew

45

Fouracre (journalist)'. I added my address, and the telephone number of both my local pub and the office. Then I posted my short story to *The People*, a racy broadsheet in those days, with a predilection for human-interest.

That was on the Wednesday. I heard nothing more until the Saturday morning, when the phone in the corner cubicle of the subs' room rang. Cherry was nearest and answered it. He came out and stayed looking at me in undisguised displeasure for a good twenty seconds, without saying a word. Then he pointedly said: '*The People* newspaper in London want a word with you.' It was quite awful. Had I been naive in giving them the office number? Perhaps in my ignorance I didn't think national newspapers ever came back with queries.

I squeezed into the cubicle and awkwardly shut the door, knowing that everyone was watching me. 'Ah, hello, old boy. *People* newsroom, here. Like your story. But just one or two points, in case we decide to use.' He suggested I might have another quick word with Mr Ricketts.

I was a flustered sixteen-year-old but feeling like a small boy caught red-handed in the guilt-ridden act of pinching apples. I suspected that half the subs had their ears pressed against the door of the cubicle. That chummy Home Counties voice wouldn't go away. Hello, old boy. . .*People* newsroom here. . . Like your story. . . The emotional amalgam was excitement and panic. He asked me to ring back in the next hour or so – and I nodded weakly, as if the fearful motion could be seen in distant EC4. I put the phone down and just sat in the little box. One naive copy boy rather wished he was back in the sixth form.

The office closed at noon on a Saturday and until then, despite intermittent looks of reprimand and even distaste, nothing more was said to me about the phone call from a brash Sunday paper. My mentor's eloquent silence added to my unease.

I retreated to the lavatory and studied my notebook again in an unavailing search for augmented information and more pearls from the gloomy Ricketts pair. So I embroidered just a fraction; I surprised myself by the apposite additional comments that drifted in from my imagination. It was no time, as a raw trainee journalist, to start contemplating newspaper ethics but I consoled myself with the belief that the new 'facts' were pretty innocuous. I hurried to the public phone box and called back *The People*. I read over my requested quotes in as mature a voice as possible. 'Thanks, old boy.

Good of you to see this Ricketts bloke again. Should be fine now. You going to be around if we need you again, just in case?' I said I'd be at home – and I prayed they wouldn't need me. But they did.

'Bad day for news and they're getting very enthusiastic about your story. The news editor wants me to blow it up a bit more.'

By now the whole thing seemed to be turning into a parody for me. It was like a film about a reporter I'd once seen. But I was finding myself bang in the middle, confused, not being able to cope, remembering things that hadn't happened, involuntarily agreeing when manufactured quotes were put to me. All the time I was being reassured by that glib, convivial Home Counties voice. 'We can work this into a really nice piece, old boy. Don't worry, – no-one will be upset.'

My mother brought *The People* to me in bed on the Sunday morning. It was front page. The headline was FIFTY YEARS LOST LOVE, which appeared to me to have a loaded and misplaced sexual connotation. I read the lengthy story, recognising the names and Mr and Mrs-to-be Ricketts and absolutely nothing else. It was very readable stuff – but it wasn't about the elderly couple I had interviewed in Goldcroft.

I sat between my parents in church for Matins and prayed hard for forgiveness. Even more impassioned were my prayers that Cherry would never discover my full part in the subterfuge and that *The People* would not find its way into the home of Mr Ricketts.

My discomfort on the Monday was a matter of some amusement to my older colleagues, maybe less than pleased that I had beaten them to the Sunday pay-cheque. They came back from coffee at the Cadena to say that a junior from the *Evening Post* had called to see Mr Ricketts in an effort to follow up the front page purple prose. He was greeted by a tirade all about flying writs and the intention to tear a pasty-faced whipper-snapper from the *Gazette*, the only person this supposed ageing Romeo had talked to, 'limb from limb'.

Sunday papers don't usually start work until the Tuesday and *The People* wasted no time in phoning me, again to my horror at the office. It was the news editor. In a manner of mock innocence, of the pitch and tenor I was to become so used to in later years as newspapers conveniently forget their indiscretions, he told me that they had received 'a very angry' letter from a firm of Yeovil solicitors. They had listed numerous disputed statements in the story and were giving notice of legal action. 'I don't know what all the fuss is about, old man. We took your story in good faith. Perhaps you can send us your notes – our lawyer will want to see them. And perhaps you can make just a couple of very small amendments. . .'

He dictated where I might make the changes. I didn't like them at all and ignored this confidential instruction. Nor was I happy, however ingenuous I might be, about the subtle way this man from a national newspaper appeared to be shifting the blame back to me.

I spent the whole of that week coping with the excessive activities of my bowels. My plight was now general knowledge. Cherry shook his head every time he passed me. We also had several fraught interviews when left together in corners of the subs' room. 'How many times, young Matthew, have I told you never to have anything to do with these so-called Sunday newspapers?' He paused for that prelude of reproach to sink in. 'And you know that we don't really allow it. I wouldn't like to think what the editor will say.'

'But, Mr Chapman, I only gave them the bare facts when they came onto me. I didn't write that story.' I was on the defensive and it made sense to leave him wondering whether someone else had leaked the whole thing, even perhaps that resourceful council workman with the shovel.

On the following Sunday, a long and comprehensive retraction appeared on the front page of *The People*, occupying roughly the same position as the original story. It began: 'There seems to have been a misunderstanding in our article. . .' And it ended: 'The couple have taken exception to this article and its heading FIFTY YEARS LOST LOVE, and, in face of these facts, we offer our apologies for any embarrassment caused by the inaccuracies in our report.'

In between was a list of those inaccuracies with the necessary corrections. There was mention in the original piece of toasting those years of lost love, of raising glasses and other references to celebratory strong drink. The retraction made it very plain indeed that Mr and Mrs Ricketts were abstainers.

For some time it looked as though my job might be in jeopardy. I took on a new zeal in my visits to Mrs Perkins and her ginger toms and over the next few weeks was subserviently dutiful around the editorial office. I had no stomach for any more immediate freelance enterprises and gave potential Sunday paymasters a wide berth. Mr Ricketts, meanwhile, was in no mood to forgive. All the rumours, gleefully relayed to me by older and smug colleagues, suggested that he had become quite paranoiac about the unwelcome publicity. He had narrowed his list of suspects, those who might have informed *The People*, down to one. There was more talk of physical threats. I decided that although he might be seventy, he possibly had relatives with broader shoulders and an even glummer expression than his. It was hard to reconcile his belligerent attitude with those scriptural texts framed around his walls.

He finally insisted on having an interview with the editor of the *Gazette*, as if the fibs in the Sunday paper were any concern of his; he made it clear he wanted to determine the extent of my role in the saga. It was arranged for him to come in one Friday afternoon, when the editor would be away and Mr Chapman would be on his day off. Clev deputised and withstood a fusillade of invective which went on unabated for nearly an hour. In an act of infinite kindness and tact, Clev had sent me off to the village of Marston Magna on the pretext of picking up whist drive winners from the night before. Mr Ricketts was told: 'Oh dear, so unfortunate for you both. But, well, these things happen. I can't believe the tip came from one of our own trusted staff.' The complainant eventually stormed out, in no way convinced.

The editor broached the ghastly subject one morning when I took in his copy of *The Times*. 'Do you know, young man, we've never had a single libel action all the years I've been editor here. And we don't like our staff getting involved in Fleet Street's sordid goings-on. I hope you have learned your lesson.' Then rapidly changing the subject as if anxious to give me new hope, he said: 'There's a real chance coming up for you tomorrow – you can show us what you can do. . .' He paused and I waited, grateful for the relaunch of a career which had so nearly been stifled at birth. 'Do you remember I promised you could cover the Rotary Club one week? You shall come with Mr Chapman and myself tomorrow. Appearance is so important when you are on official duties for this paper – I shall expect you to wear a suit.'

On the way home, I called into Cyril's gents' hairdressing saloon. He was a gossip and a rural philosopher. He'd impart a malicious morsel, gleaned from an earlier customer, and then ponder aloud the profounder implications. He cut hair at his own unforced pace, irrespective of how many of his good-natured cronies and neighbours were waiting their turn for the somnolent scissors. Whenever a car passed, or so it seemed, he would go to the window – and then relay to the rest of us the make of the machine, the number of occupants and the likely destination. He stacked a teetering pile of dog-eared Sunday papers on the arm of a faded Edwardian settee, through which the springs protruded. I averted my eyes in case there was evidence of my recent creative excesses.

The saloon smelt seductively of Denis Compton's brylcreem and the cheap brilliantine used in the spray which everyone requested as the remaining hair was slammed down. You didn't go to Cyril's for the subtleties of coiffure, more for the gossip. That evening I paid my 1s 6d for the conventional back-and-sides and resolved I'd one day ask what exactly you got for a 9d singe, a service prominently advertised but not, as far as I could see, ever patronised.

I felt tidier about the back of the neck. The next day my brown pinstripe suit was proudly retrieved from the communal wardrobe by my mother. I was ready for the Rotary Club. Mr Chapman gave me several approving sideway glances; he looked even cleaner and pinker than usual. He always looked forward to the Tuesday lunch.

The editor peered round the door at 12.30pm. Then the three of us walked, abreast, up Middle Street to the Cadena. The editor and his assistant both carried a rolled umbrella. I carried, just a little ostentatiously, my reporter's notebook.

'This will be a useful experience for you, young man. An interesting speaker but he won't yield too much copy. Maybe a stick and a half,' said my editor. 'Stick' was the printers' measure we always used within the office. It meant twenty lines or so of 8-point type; in those days if we had talked about three inches of copy we'd have been branded as phoneys.

The meal was bland, heralded by the ubiquitous and dreadful Brown Windsor which, I got the impression, was being pumped up during the war years and just after from an inexhaustible muddy reservoir deep underground. The toast of 'Rotary round the World' was drunk – in water. Everything was desperately polite and formal; little conclaves of elderly men on various tables seemed engrossed in the current prices of furniture, ironmongery or shorthorns, influenced by the dominant Rotarian within that group. The Church and the Council were both well represented at the lunch. The president wore his chain and elicited rounds of gentle applause as he introduced the guests. Most of them were rather self-satisfied pillars of commercial respectability from neighbouring towns. The youngest member of the *Gazette's* editorial staff didn't earn a mention.

Then it came to the speaker. His subject was 'The Electronic Structure of Matter'. He read from a typescript, without the relief of a light-hearted dalliance or any variation of tone. He went on, as invited, for thirty minutes. There were no questions.

On the brisk walk back to the office, the editor amended his earlier advice. 'Not at all a bad speaker,' he said, to my astonishment, 'but not quite right for us. Too technical. Make it half a stick.' Mr Chapman, taking long, unnatural strides and using his umbrella as a walking stick as he struggled to keep up, added: 'But don't forget to say who proposed a vote of thanks. . . Mr Mogson from the Fish and Poultry shop. A good friend of ours. Always used to take a big display advertisement at Christmas time in the *Gazette* before the war. . .'

I'd filled six pages of my notebook with meaningless jargon. I gave the longhand no more than a cursory glance. Half a stick of that was generous editorial treatment.

Half a stick from the stuffy old Rotarians – and not even the fleeting sight of Diana, doubtless relegated to service at the lower level of the restaurant. She just wouldn't have been right ladling out the Brown Windsor to the town's primly suited business establishment.

I knocked out my report in a minute flat. That included the vote of thanks which took up three lines. It was all a bit flat after threatened libel actions.

Mr and Mrs Ricketts received an out-of-court settlement. I waited two months and then got my cheque from *The People*. It came to three guineas, hardly worth the trouble.

But the next time I went to Cyril's for a haircut, some of the bravado and romantic fantasy had returned. I pointed to the pile of old Sunday papers on the rickety arm of the settee. 'Do a bit myself, Cyril, for some of those. Got a nice story in *The People* the other week, don't know if you saw it. Always glad to hear from you if you run across a good story. . .'

FOUR

A Ride with the Dead

I T SOON STRUCK ME that 'death' was the lifeblood of the *Western Gazette*. The columns were filled with glowing obituaries – even if the phrasing was stylised and repetitive – and interminable lists of mourners at the funeral services. The single-column headlines changed marginally: 'Death of well-known seed merchant' . . . 'Tributes to well-known parish councillor' . . . 'Well-known Women's Institute president mourned' . . . Could there really be so many people well known, I used to ask myself?

'We think it's time to send you out on the cemetery calls this Tuesday morning. Young Gerald will tell you what you've got to do,' I was told.

Young Gerald, by now a bosom mate as he regaled me with embroidered accounts of the previous night's explorative liaisons, was more than happy for me to take over the cemetery calls. He'd been sated with the ritual for too long and was ready to return to the world of the living. 'Old Johnson is a nice bloke,' Gerald assured me. 'Looks a bit like the back of a hearse but he'll give you all the facts.'

Ah yes, the facts. That had an authentic ring – if not quite off the pages of Gibbs' *Street of Adventure* then at least from one of those stacked ledgers in Mr Johnson's cemetery cottage.

He was the superintendent, a small man with squinting eyes and a back prematurely inclined to stoop like some of those misshapen tombstones visible from his office window. He always wore a faded grey suit and had the gentle-voiced manner that was a prerequisite of the job. He spent his days talking in melancholy tones to mourning relatives or undertakers whose businessmen's eyes sparkled bright as the polished coffin handles whenever trade was at its briskest.

I introduced myself to Mr Johnson on the following morning, explaining that I'd taken over from Gerald and did he have some names for me? He always had, of course. There were seven for me – and two more if I cared to phone up later in the day. They made up the town's dead since the last batch had been catalogued in the columns of the WG.

My notebook was flourished. There were names and addresses, ages and occupations to be taken down. I was given the date of death and of the looming funeral. An occasional observation was also offered, for my ears rather than notebook. 'Been going for the last three years. It was the cider, you know. They say only a quarter of his liver was still there.' Or: 'He was a funny old bugger. You must have seen him walking up and down Hendford Hill in his pork-pie hat. Mad as a hatter. Never done a day's work in his life. . .'

I would use Mrs Perkins' shorthand for the odd word, leaving the notebook at such an angle that Mr Johnson could see and admire. The cemetery call was an unsentimental duty for me. It got me out of the office. I would chat knowledgeably about Yeovil Town FC with the lugubrious superintendent and then with some nonchalance light a Players Weight as I began my cycle ride back to the office.

A few families sent in their own reports. But the routine for whoever did the cemetery call was to return to the office with the list of names before setting off, over the next day or so, to see all the surviving widows, widowers, sons and daughters. Very few of the families were on the phone in those days. You just knocked at the door, offered a stumbling word of sympathy and then invited the weeping dependants to pass on the intimate details for public consumption.

Over the next year or so I knocked on hundreds of doors. I learned to do the job in a dispassionate and efficient way. I faltered and hesitated over the call only when I knew the family. Another set of emotions and perceptions then seemed to take over. I never quite understood, and still don't the chemical process that brought the tears.

The write-up which followed my visits was bald and mechanical. Mrs Morgan would be described as 'a well-respected member of the Methodist Church' or maybe 'a former chairman of the flower show committee'. There were no frills. None of the lovely anecdotes, passed on by doting relatives, that would have lent colour, humour and even nobility to the dear departed were ever allowed past the sub-editor's pencil.

With the rarest exceptions, the surviving relatives were helpful and welcoming. They accepted that it was part of the last rites to have one or two appropriate paragraphs in the local paper. It gave a certain dignity and stature to what had perhaps been a mundane and almost anonymous life. Those relatives put the kettle on as they passed on the basic biographical details with affectionate simplicity. They took me into their confidence, showing me the pot plants, the sepia snapshots and the shared mementos as they did so. This was a valid part of my self-education, far more valuable than a university course in psychology.

There were, of course, the delicate moments. 'Well, I know I can tell you. . . just you. But it weren't only me. He had a fancy woman. Two kids from her, too. That's four of mine and two of hers. They'll all be coming to the funeral. Don't know how we can put that.' We usually found a way.

And the suicides. I had several of them. The family would start by pretending it was all a normal death and I didn't need to know. Then came the unintended admission – and the needless guilt.

Some took a pragmatic, philosophical approach. There was the middle-aged husband whose wife, in depression, had swallowed aspirins to kill herself. The husband was distraught but, an officer not long out of the army, did his best to put on a Serviceman's brave face. 'What's your name? Matthew. . . Come on up to the Three Choughs and we'll have a drink together.' He clearly needed company. We searched and talked in frantic succession of almost every subject but his wife's death. There was much nervous laughter.

By an odd coincidence I had been reading just before a biography of Richard Doddridge Blackmore, the author of *Lorna Doone*. The Three Choughs had come into that story. Trying to be as matter-of-fact as my older companion, and failing badly with my lack of tact, I asked him whether he knew that Blackmore's eccentric brother, Henry, had committed suicide in that same Yeovil hotel. In an attempt to mitigate my insensitivity, I said: 'But no-one was quite sure whether it was suicide, whatever the coroner said. Richard was convinced it was murder – and he ended up with some libel writs he could have done without.' We had a little discussion about sibling loyalty and there was more nervous laughter.

In the middle of a sentence, he broke off. 'It's so wrong, so unfair. I should have been killed a dozen times in the war. I got through it somehow and now I was looking forward to a proper and happy married life at last. But dear Rosemary was killed by an enemy inside her head.' It sounds at this distance corny and melodramatic. In the public bar of the Three Choughs he burst uncontrollably into tears.

I found myself crying as well and putting my arm on his shoulder, as a son would if his father were in distress. It was the only time in my duties as the cemetery correspondent that I cried.

He quickly recovered, embarrassed, and changed the subject. We shook hands and he invited me back for tea and 'a proper drink' after the funeral. It had been a warm and rewarding half-hour in the Three Choughs. I wasn't sent to the funeral and I never saw the husband again.

In the lunch hours I normally retired with my sandwich box to a small storeroom I found by accident along the corridor from the subs' sanctum. It was an isolated cubby-hole, perfect for reflection and fantasy, both of which were prone to be liberally interwoven into my workaday life as a hamstrung copy boy.

The subs went home most lunchtimes so I was able to steal away with copies of *The Times*, the *Manchester Guardian* and the *Express* (I could see the *Mail* and the beloved *News Chronicle* at home). That was private bliss, interrupted only when I heard the high heels or platforms rattling up the stairs and when I caught the first, imagined whiffs of exotic south Somerset scent.

Death must have been for me at that time something of an enforced obsession. In that same storeroom, lit by a single naked bulb, I read all the national obituaries: of prewar sporting heroes, of Damon Runyan and H.G. Wells, whose brief schoolteaching links with Wookey Hole, in Somerset, came as a surprise to me – as did the fact that his father, a small shopkeeper, had also been a professional cricketer with Kent.

The Nuremberg Trials were read avidly by me. It was disquieting and depressing stuff for a sixteen-year-old, anxious to forget all about the war. Much of the evidence had a chilling effect on me. Then came the ten initial sentences of execution, to be carried out in Nuremberg Prison – and Goering's suicide a few hours before he was due to die. And there were the words of the judges that many of the twenty-two defendants had shown great dignity during the trials. This filled me with a strange, troubling ambivalence: thoughts of revenge, retribution and forgiveness all tangled up. I was sickened by the catalogue of evil, yet didn't want to be reminded of it. At the same time I was confused by the apparent image of civilised, dignified men with quiet voices, now asking in vain for mercy. I was glad I didn't have to apportion the blame.

As I did my best to form mature judgments in the store cupboard, so I bit with symbolic savagery into my blackcurrant sandwiches. There were always six big slices, artistically cut into triangles by my mother. I didn't know how she did it. The 2lb loaf was now down to 1¾lb with no reduction in price. But she worked on the countrywomen's axiom that you needed plenty of good basic grain to keep the cold out, especially when you had to cycle four miles in the morning to work, before it got light.

There was no apparent decline in Yeovil's mortality rate. Mr Johnson continued with his gossipy reveries as each week he looked out at the timeless, beckoning tombstones. 'You and I'll be there one day, propping up them daisies. A nice headstone, that's all you need. Got some good monumental masons round here, you know. They do a nice job for you.' It was always bright conversation.

I got to know the various undertakers. All of them had wan complexions and, I suspected, well-stacked wallets. 'Don't forget the paragraph at the end' they'd say. They were talking about the two lines tacked on after the list of mourners, to indicate which firm had carried out the funeral arrangements.

I could see no imminent extension of my embryonic journalism so had to make the best of my obit-writing. There were always the unexpected pearls to heighten my interest. I could never be certain what diverse life story would be revealed after I knocked on the door of a drab terrace house or country cottage. My imagination was much stirred, for instance, by the case of Alfred James Walden. 'Old bloke, aged eighty-one. Don't know much about him – but a bit of a singer in his younger days,' I was vaguely told. It was an inadequate briefing.

From his widow, his second wife, emerged a career of fleeting fame and unfulfilled talent. Alf Walden had been a songwriter, a prolific one whose hearty music-hall ditties had been peddled round the music publishers of his day. He wrote under the name of Harry Wincott; his songs were commissioned, or at least used, by Marie Lloyd, Harry Champion and many of their extrovert contemporaries. There were so many. He churned them out to order – and got a pittance. There were meagre royalties and few scruples. Today, boosted by the charts, he would have been a millionaire. The pattern of popular music changed and Harry Wincott was forgotten. There was tragedy in his private life and he died a poor man. I listened spellbound, saddened by the apathy of a fickle public.

'Alfie came out of retirement just before he was eighty, you know. He took part in one of the 'victory' concerts in the town. He was very fond of Yeovil, happier than he'd been for years.' I wished I could have seen that final concert. I wished I could have written a whole column about Harry Wincott.

I always got on pretty well with the gipsies. There weren't so many of the genuine old Romany caravans around but you would still occasionally see one on the wide grass verge of a country lane and pause momentarily, half in wonderment and half in fear, to sniff in romantic envy the smoke from the crackling log fire at the foot of the caravan steps. They were always being moved on by the police. We grew up to believe, too often without question, that they were dirty and dishonest. The women, with their leathery faces and hooked noses, all looked alike to me. They kept knocking at our cottage door, trying to sell clothes-pegs. My mother would see them coming up the path and say: 'You go, Matthew. But don't you go buying any of them clothes-pegs or bunches of heather.'

The spiel could become quite frightening. First came the offer of newly cut pegs. 'Never wear out or break, mister. Lovely pegs for yer ma's washin'. Cut 'em only yesterday, mister.' If there was no obvious response, the heather was proffered. 'Bring you luck, mister. Buy a bunch of this special heather and you'll be lucky fer evermore. And yer ma will.' The women usually came in twos to the door. If you still made no effort to reach for your purse, the second woman would come in with an air of desperation. 'The heather, me dear, is a lucky charm. Fer just sixpence. Buy just this one bunch and yer'll have no bad luck, no rheumatics, no deaths in the family. . . no spots.' Clever so-and-so: she must have detected the early threats of adolescent acne.

They were bad losers. When there was no prospect at all of a sale after ten minutes of rasping blandishments, they would trudge away with an audible curse on the family.

I relished their naive, inexpert methods of salesmanship, made up of plea, smarm and blackmail. I never once saw any of them smile; often I was left on the doorstep as they withdrew into intense patois before changing the style and direction of their approach. Once or twice I bought the heather after some perfunctory bargaining. My mother never really approved. 'You don't know where it's been', she would say with sweeping finality. It may have been the supernatural threats that bothered her more.

Their menfolk stayed in the caravans or in the waggons out in the road. It was a sexist structure. But I knew that the men, apart from being adept at pony trading and detecting the distant approaches of the village constable, had prodigious thirsts. It was often evident on market day in Yeovil, where the pubs stayed open longer and the gipsies were welcome at certain inns just as long as they remained in good humour and demonstrated that there were still crisp ten shilling notes to be extracted from the inside pocket.

Several times in court, as I waited to deliver edition-day copy back to the office, I was transfixed when gipsies were fined for poaching or other transgressions of the byways. Vast piles of mint-new notes would be produced from the inner recesses of those torn, loose-hanging jackets. They saw no point in depositing their monetary accumulations in the bank.

It was from one of the leather-faced callers at my parents' cottage that I heard about the death of old Anna Light. 'She's our Queen, me lovely. Queen o' all our tribe. Thousands there'll be at the funeral in Yeovil. From all over England they be comin'. Tis sad fer us all.'

There weren't in truth thousands but well over eight hundred at the funeral. The office had told me I could cover it, as it was on a Friday, our quietest day. 'Just a straight report, young Matthew. Nothing fancy.' And as a perceptive afterthought: 'Gipsies don't buy papers, remember.'

Rowly overheard the remark. 'Lazy buggers. Just tell me how many of 'em fought in the war. Better if they paid their bloody rates like the rest of us – instead of nicking all the daffs every spring.' Nothing like a bit of unmitigated bigotry after a night on the Bass.

I got to the cemetery early. From dawn the gipsies had been converging on the town. By the time of the service, they had marshalled themselves uncannily into a long, snaking, silent line. The order was determined by seniority within the tribe. No-one appeared to say anything; they just knew by instinct where they had to stand. Only the immediate relatives of old Anna Light walked into the chapel. The men, five or six hundred of them, were already bareheaded. Their caps were stuffed into their commodious poachers' pockets.

The family came out of the chapel and followed the coffin to the graveside. There were dozens of ornate wreaths, and many sprays plucked fresh from the hedgerows that morning, to be thrown reverentially, deep into the grave on top of the oaken box.

By now there was a crescendo of private prayers and incantations. The new Queen, sister Nellar, was steadied by two men as she looked in for the last time; then she was led away. Over the next hour, all eight hundred or so mourners filed past, many of them mumbling their final message to their late leader. I found it both moving and eerie.

I stood back, very much a stranger. When the cemetery was at last nearly deserted, half a dozen men stood in a circle round the grave. The rain glistened on their gnarled features. A new ritual was clearly about to be performed. They said nothing but the oldest member of the tribe suddenly brandished a bottle of beer. He took a long swig, after lifting the metal top with his teeth. The bottle was then passed from gipsy to gipsy. I crept away and, in the road outside, diffidently asked the meaning of that particular ceremony. 'That often happens, child. The past can't be changed. Life goes on, child. Our menfolk are drinkin' to the future Queen.'

There was more I wanted to ask. Would the old Queen's caravan be burned? It was a snippet of unreliable Romany legend I had acquired from a source in the office. 'No, child. All Anna's possessions, they be burned. Gone fer ever. But not the caravan. Tha's Nellar's now.'

I went back to the office to write my report. It just couldn't start with: 'The funeral took place. . .' Not this one. I put my piece of lavatory-white copy paper in the typewriter and defiantly banged out my intro: 'Strange gipsy rites were performed at the Yeovil funeral of Mrs Anna Light, beloved 'queen' of her tribe. . .'

To my joy it went in like that the following Friday. It made my head buzz with pride. Could I even be changing the pattern of more than two hundred years? Just wait till they let me loose on the next meeting of the Rotary.

But the truth was I was now stuck with funerals. I shivered in church porches as I dutifully took down military ranks, double-barrelled names and a thousand permutations of initials that I got wrong at my peril. Some formidable mourners would push visiting cards in my numbed fingers, with a challenging: 'Not likely to get it wrong this way, what?' Patronising sods, I thought.

Cherry was evidently pleased with my proficiency in getting down long, dreary columns of people's names, while signifying whether they were representing the local gospel hall or the Old Comrades Association. 'You are coming along nicely, young man.' He could have fooled me.

Mr Chapman had a disconcerting habit of pointing, leaving the arm extended for up to twenty seconds before he made his statement. I wondered what the summons might be this time, even though the theatrical arm movement was generously used even when I was about to be dispatched to buy ten Players from across the road.

'Do you think you are ready to go away from Yeovil? I've a good job lined up for you tomorrow. It's an important story for the

Gazette. But we're short of staff and I'm going to give you your head on this one. Make sure you have your bicycle with you tomorrow.' I nodded, overcome by the responsibilities being vested in me.

He went on, smiling with unsmiling lips: 'Have you any idea where Charlton Mackrell is?'

I wasn't too sure but expressed fitting confidence. Ignorance over local geography was an unforgivable sin at the WG.

'You aren't confusing it with Charlton Horethorne, are you? Or Charlton Musgrove? Charlton Mackrell is also in Somerset.' He enjoyed the joke and laughed out loud. No, I wasn't, I said, pleasing him by returning the laugh.

'Right, then. I want you to take down everything I am now going to tell you. In shorthand if you can. Don't get anything wrong. Now tomorrow there is a big funeral at Charlton Mackrell at 2.30. Miss Emily Pomeroy. . . P for Peter. . . O. . . M for Mother. . .EROY. Have you got that? Good. A pillar of the church and local community' (it was as if Mr Chapman was already dictating my report for me). 'There will be a lot of mourners. You will need to be at the church forty-five minutes at least before the service starts. Don't miss anyone. Every name, every initial.' He suddenly looked at the yellow tie I was wearing. 'And maybe a more sober colour would be appropriate tomorrow, don't you think?'

I checked the direction next day with Buzz and cycled off towards Ilchester. That was only about halfway and I realised with some concern that the church was farther away than I had imagined. The wind was against me and there was a drizzle blowing into my face. My trilby wouldn't stay on; after retrieving it from a puddle, I determined never to wear it again, at least not until I got to Fleet Street.

At last I came to a sign post, marked 'Charlton Mackrell', pointing ominously up a narrow country road. By now I was thoroughly wet and uncomfortable. I feared that the pages of my notebook were sodden. And then my misery was compounded when my cycle began to bump and lurch on the unkempt road. It very soon dawned on me that I had a fast puncture in my front tyre.

I wasn't at all sure how near I was to the church but I sensed that my chances of making contact with any mourners on the exterior side of the porch were decreasing by the minute. I threw my faithful but wounded racer against an elm trunk. It was a time for drastic decision – though I couldn't quite think what. I started to run.

Almost at once I heard the sound of some kind of traffic behind me. This had to be my opening lesson in journalistic resourcefulness. I stood in the middle of the narrow road and thumbed down the driver.

The rain dripping down from my tangled hair partly obscured my vision. But it didn't take me long to realise the enormity of my blunder. For I had stopped the hearse. I was vaguely aware of another car with a few occupants behind.

The driver of the hearse poked his head out of the window, tilting back his battered, almost comic, peaked cap as he did so. 'What's the trouble, lad? We've a burial to catch. And we've got the body inside.'

An undertaker's assistant with a sense of humour offered a glimmer of hope. What alternative was there, in any case? 'Dreadful thing's happened. Just had a puncture – and I've got to get to the church in time. I'm from the *Gazette*.'

'Climb in. Here, Bill, move over. The lad's got to get to the church on time.' He hummed the appropriate sentimental song as I squeezed in alongside them. 'That makes the four of us. A nice number. Us three – and the body. The other bearers will be waiting for us at the farm. We drop 'em off afterwards to do the milking. They keep their dark suits in the cow shed.'

The hearse chugged along the rough country road at a respectful pace. I had started to dry myself with my big white pocket handkerchief. There was time for some panicky contemplation. If I didn't get to the church before the coffin, what chance did I have of taking all those names? The driver interrupted my troubled train of thought.

'Surprised the *Gazette* is bothering with thissin.'

He shouldn't have been, I felt. 'Oh, I understand this is a really big funeral. A lot of people coming.'

'I don't think so, lad. Just two or three of the family. And they're in the Austin 7 behind. Poor old Herbie Masters has been past it for years. Nobody remembers him no more. Tha's what's sad about old age.'

'Herbie. . .?'

'Tha's it, laddie. Herbert Ambrose Masters, aged ninety-one. Funeral Charlton Adam Church, 2.15pm, Tuesday.'

My heart was pounding. Was there really a Charlton Adam, as well?

'Oh dear, sorry. Can I get out? Where's Charlton Mackrell, please? That's where I should be.'

The driver retained his jocular manner. 'So many Charltons, inn't there? Could have been worse for you, though. Could have been bloody Charlton Athletic!' He was now irritating me, but he continued: 'Look out across that hedgerow, by this gate. There 'tis. Next village. But 'fraid I can't take you all the way. Old Herbie were an Adam man.' Another little chuckle.

I stammered my thanks and left the other three occupants, including the lamented and long-forgotten Mr Masters. I ran back to the five-bar gate and looked across in the direction of Charlton Mackrell Church. It didn't seem quite so far that way. I climbed over the gate and headed across the middle of a field. Not quite as the crow flies – more like the way an anxious, soaked cub reporter stumbles.

The rough, undulating meadowland squelched as I planted one weary leg after another. My shoe stuck in the liquid mud of a cattle track and rapidly subsided out of sight. It was retrieved with heaving difficulty. But in a sort of benumbed state I started running again; the whole ghastly exercise brought back memories of hideous school cross-country runs that had been fiendishly choreographed through a sewage farm. I struggled over yet another five-bar gate and dropped onto the road, not so far from the church. I could see the cars parked on the grass verge – and the cycles stacked against the wall of the churchyard. It looked like dozens of them. But not a human soul in sight. Oh no, not yet another wrong place of worship! Was the *Gazette* going to fail to pay its last column-filling respects to the esteemed Miss Pomeroy?

Then as I reached the church door I heard the vicar. His doleful voice wafted out to me. 'Miss Pomeroy was indeed a pillar of the Church and the local community. . .' (Hey, had Mr Chapman written his script, I asked myself?) 'She represented our finest values – of nobility of manner, of service to her fellow man. . . It is only right that her rich and fruitful life on this earth should be remembered and recorded for all to admire and wish to emulate.'

Record, did he say? The chances of anything being recorded for posterity looked bleak to me. I peered through the wide glass panelling of the inner church door. The intimate parish church was packed. And I estimated they were well into the funeral service: without a single name in the sodden notebook.

Cold logic took over. I calculated that there was absolutely no chance of collecting any names once the service was over and the mourners were departing in all directions, keen to get out of the driving rain as quickly as possible. So I pursued my logic of spontaneous enterprise. I crept into the church, obscured by a Norman pillar, from the view of the vicar. I tore out several sheets of relatively dry paper from the middle of my notebook. On the top I printed: 'List of mourners for official purposes – please write your name and whom you represent.' There were always numerous stubs of pencil in my pocket; I handed a sheet of paper and a stub to mourners sitting nearest to me, on the ends of pews. With an imperious, affectedly confident gesture, I indicated that the paper should be systematically passed along the row. The members of the congregation tugged at their black ties or navy blue scarves. They gave me quizzical looks, some seemingly irritated that such pragmatic matters should be allowed to conflict with the clerical eulogy. But they complied.

The vicar, conscious of a captive congregation and very much in awe of Miss Pomeroy's standing in the parish, went on at great length. Meanwhile with an organisational skill I didn't know I possessed, I moved along the rows like a sidesman with an offertory plate. My presence had, by this time, caused a minor stir. A bedraggled youth, his trouser bottoms plastered in mud and rain still trickling down his cheeks, must have been a diversion to the solemnity of the occasion. Twice the vicar looked up, pausing as if to speak and maybe reprimand. But he continued with his homily, which he had prepared with such punctilious and verbose care.

I sidled all the way down one side of the nave and, as they went into the last hymn, I slipped across to the central aisle. By now I must have stuffed thirty or so sheets of lined paper into my breast pocket.

The practical, unspoken process continued. I was gratified at the measure of co-operation but by now some must have guessed at the reason for my mission and a natural inclination to see their name in the paper had outweighed their concern over the irregularities of my approach. This was a foible of human nature that I was to recognise and exploit so often in the years that followed.

Almost comically, I went on forcing successive scraps of damp paper into my top pocket. It was no time to worry about the legibility of the writing. The reassuring fact was that I actually had some names. . . dozens of them. By now, impervious from necessity to the embarrassment of intruding on private and public grief and unmindful of the parson's recurrent glances of mounting outrage, I was prominently poised in the central aisle, only a pew or so behind the three rows of dark-suited family. The hymn finished earlier than I would have wished and the vicar went into his final prayers and blessing. I was stranded, the only occupant in the church, apart from the reverent gentleman, left on his feet.

The congregation murmured their collective Amens and the undertaker nodded to his bearers. They moved forward, expertly heaving the oak coffin up onto their broad countrymen's shoulders. Then they began to carry the body back out of the church.

The undertaker and the vicar walked first. I glanced up and saw those half dozen broad-shouldered countrymen bearing down on me. Their expressions were suitably pious. They seemed oblivious to my plight. The undertaker had narrow eyes, with none of the innate humour I'd detected during my earlier experience on board a hearse. The vicar also brushed past, shooting me the kind of manifestly uncharitable look that I am sure was never taught at theological college.

To me it was almost a matter of physical survival as the lofted coffin and its hefty henchmen-bearers loomed with ominous inevitability. My note-taking was clearly over. In one spontaneous movement, as I summoned up an apposite show of dignity, I pocketed my book, turned and joined the procession as it shuffled out to the west door. Well, not so much joined as *headed*: just the two officials in front of me. Then came the body, the weeping relatives and, as they filed out of their pews, two or three hundred villagers and friends.

With sedate, measured steps we walked through the drizzle to the graveside for the interment. I remained in a position of mysterious eminence. It must have looked very much as if I had a role of some family substance. Hedged in and hapless I may have been back in the church; now I found myself drawn emotionally into the final rites. I closed my eyes for the prayers and uttered my Amens in a firm bass voice as befitted perhaps a principal beneficiary.

The realisation that I was in effect an interloper returned. Once again I pondered my predicament; my obvious stratagem had to be to make my churchyard getaway with as much stealth as possible before I became integrated in the converging mourners with their mutual sentiments of sympathy.

I pulled the soaked pocket handkerchief out one last time to dry my face and dripping eyebrows.

'We all feel like that. There's no shame in tears. You must have been close to the good lady.'

A grey-haired mourner shielded me with his umbrella. It seemed insensitive of me to ruin the illusion of shared sympathy and affection for Miss Pomeroy. 'So many loved her. She was very much part of Charlton Mackrell,' I said in phoney compromise. The pair of us fell silent, nodding our heads. Maybe it was time to come clean, I thought. 'Actually, I'm here from the *Western Gazette.*'

His reaction filled me with renewed hope. 'Oh wonderful, wonderful. We didn't think anyone was here. You took the names as they all came in, did you?'

'Em – yes. A great many at the service. I daresay a few slipped through but I got most of them. Nearly a notebook full.'

The middle-aged mourner patted me on the back. 'The family will be so pleased. You must come back to the Priory for a cup of tea – we can give you the complete list of family mourners at the same time. Now, let me see, how can we arrange a ride for you? Did you come out to Mackrell on the bus?'

I explained no, on my cycle which at the moment was lying in a deflated state against an elm tree at least a mile and a half away.

My kindly companion spoke to the undertaker and returned to me. 'I do hope you aren't superstitious. You will be hitching a lift in the empty hearse back to the Priory. And we shall arrange for Miss Pomeroy's gardener to pick up your cycle.'

The ride back to the elegant old house was carried out in icy silence. There were no pleasantries from the undertaker who sat alongside the driver. Now that the formalities were over, he'd taken on a contrasting persona. I didn't know what had happened to that earlier decorum and subservience. A hearse without a body was, I also concluded, a singularly soulless vehicle.

At the Priory I carried the mud from my shoes onto the carpet but no-one seemed to bother. Miss Pomeroy had gone on – and she was the last of the line. The big house would be sold, no doubt. Who cared about mud on the Persian carpet?

The list of close family mourners was dictated to me as I sipped tea from bone china and nibbled at a finger of Madeira cake. The courtesies and attentions showered on me were embarrassing. 'Don't you worry about that bicycle of yours. Everything is being seen to. It's been collected in the back of a farm waggon and Jones the gardener is actually at this very minute putting a patch on the puncture. Oh dear, such a horrid day. And so good of you to come all this way. The family do appreciate it. You must have another finger of Madeira. . .'

I sank deep into an early Victorian chair of splendid upholstery. Was this what was meant by the power of the Press? Two rides in a hearse – and back to tea at the Priory. I knew in an instant why Hannen Swaffer had gone into journalism.

FIVE

Diana and a Future PM

T HE EDITOR WAS a small man of commendable integrity. He didn't upset the advertisers. Nor did he allow them free plugs. The merest attempt by a deft businessman to inveigle a mention of his expanding firm into the news columns was obliterated by a thick lead pencil. The editor also demanded, at least theoreti- cally, complete impartiality in the reporting of political meetings.

He stopped me in the dark first-floor corridor one morning. His manner was kindly. He paused, making me wonder what he was going to ask. Then: 'What are your family's politics?'

That seemed rather intrusive to me, even more so in retrospect. But I told him the truth. 'I'm – er – not too sure.' He probably made an instant judgment that my apparent reluctance to tell meant they voted Labour. The *Gazette*, whatever its independent banner, had a rich seam of Conservatism running through its history. Most of the present board, I imagined, were High Tory.

But the simple fact was that I didn't know how my father and mother voted. We never discussed politics at home. I suspected Dad might be, at least on polling day, a surreptitious socialist – in tune with the mood of social change that came in the late Forties. At times, in a philosophical aside as the pair of us hand-weeded the onion patch, he would talk inconsequentially of the Means Test before the war. It was a cruel, insensitive measure, interwoven for ever in working-class minds with the Conservative Party. Mum, I think, always voted the same way as Dad; that was the normal pattern in village life. Domestic division, when it came to polling, carried far too much guilt. I would say that my parents were basically Liberal. Lloyd George's peccadilloes wouldn't have earned approval but they still went mostly unreported. The white-haired Celt's name was mentioned with more awe in our household than that of Stanley Baldwin.

67

The editor gave me a slow, crafty smile. 'Perhaps I shouldn't have asked you, young Matthew. No business of mine. But I am so insistent that no reporter of mine allows his family's beliefs to get in the way of his journalism.' He paused again, this time to contemplate my progress. 'Has Mr Chapman put you down yet for the Party calls?'

I had to admit that he hadn't. My face acquired an undisguised longing. This latest suggestion had to be for me a refreshing alternative to the weekly cemetery ritual. 'Well, then, I think it's about time you started making them. No bias, remember.' His stern Victorian expression flickered into a little smile. 'No bias, just because this Attlee fellow is at No 10.'

My politics, in no sense articulated, were all the same imbued with a modest radical zeal. I had a vaguely romantic view of the Labour Party, moulded by the voluminous acclaim of a nation of liberated plebs back from the war. I'd been a Depression Years baby and my father later told me he couldn't afford a second child. I came to discover there was a surprising number of families in my village with one child. Dad's wages in 1939 were still only thirty-five shillings a week. Our one real cooked meal of the week was on Sunday when at least four vegetables from the garden garnished the roast. If there was a certain deprivation in rural life at my level, it struck me neither as unusual nor the reason for harbouring a grievance. When I went down with scarlet fever, the Colonel, my father's employer, sent down some calves-foot jelly from Fortnum and Mason. That seemed pretty warm-hearted to me.

Now, a worker myself for the first time, I wasn't given to analysing my emerging political feelings. I liked Attlee for his diffidence and the homely way his wife drove him in the battered saloon at election time. I knew he shared my passion for cricket; that made up for his dry, bland manner as a speaker. In fact, I veered slightly more towards Nye Bevan, because his oratory, heightened by the stammer, was so exhilarating and contentious. The vowels, too, belonged less to the public school. I was going through a minor class hang-up at the time.

On Saturdays when I wasn't working I would play football for the Yeovil League of Youth. This was in no sense a political statement. But Buzz, however spindly his legs and however suspect his reserves of energy, was holding down a place and he worked me in as well. The trainer was a Glaswegian commie. He had a bald head and a range of invective never experienced on the wholesome meadowlands of East Coker. I think you were supposed to be a Young Socialist or something similar to play for the League of Youth. Application forms were never proffered to me. The trainer may have thought we were playing for Lenin. But the more pressing consideration was to find eleven players who had their own pair of boots and a white shirt. Collective political aspirations within the side were, as far as I could make out, minimal. A few of those erstwhile players now no doubt have two cars parked on a winding, gravel drive.

The editor passed on his message and I was quickly given instructions on how to make the Party calls. I came to do them each Wednesday morning. It was unfailingly affable. Soon I was wishing I could vote for all the parties.

At the Liberal Hall, a substantial building which reflected some loyal, local allegiance to the Gladstone tradition, there was always time for a quick frame of billiards on one of the full-sized tables. I used to be told by the cynical bystanders that there were more tables than party workers. Certainly the cues were being chalked by a dozen of Yeovil's wan Joe Davises for most of the day. In the adjoining office, I was given details of coming meetings, fund-raising whist drives and everlasting claims of statistical inroads into specific country communities. 'You must cycle out to West Chinnock and take a look for yourself. We're getting a new branch going. A lot of Non-Conformists out there.'

Up the stairs, above the Unity Hall, there was always the stench of strong baccy and Bruttons bitter from the night before. The Labour agent was an energetic man with a fertile concept of news. He often had an imaginative angle to offer, though it was more likely to appeal to the evening paper reporter who had space and latitude on his side.

I was soon introduced to Joe Kelly, a warm, loquacious Irishman who worked at Westland and was chairman of the local Trades Council. Everyone liked Joe, even the Tories whom he blasphemed with the obligatory ire. It was always done without malice. 'You must come to the next Trades Council meeting,' he advised. 'That'll give you some damned good copy.'

I went along, sitting with pride behind the small trestle table that Joe had set aside for two or three of us. The evening was an Event, two hours of unmitigated vitriol: hate, outrageous slander and some raucous humour. Every employer, it appeared, was 'a bloody shit'. Joe wrestled to keep order but knew he had no real chance and capitulated with an air of unperturbed resignation. Burly trade unionists shook their fists, all shouted at once and, oblivious to the subject matter, stalked in and out of the adjoining bar in mid-monologue.

It was magnificent drama, interspersed with the occasional, incongruously gentle voice of a miming Fabian who you felt had got in by mistake. Motions were put, revised, reversed, rescinded. Speeches and interruptions veered and deviated. It was marvellous mayhem: a hotch-potch that encompassed *Itma*, Denis Compton's knee and, almost by default it seemed to me, the social and economic reforms that were transforming the nation. 'What about this hure bacon rationin'? Down to bloody three ounzes. Who do 'ee blame fer that? Them fat-bellied farmers.'

Often the wrong ones got the blame. The Americans, I fancied, were blamed for most things. 'What chance have us got with they Yanks screwin' us? Just think of the terms this bloke Keynes have had to settle fer on this latest bloody loan. But what do 'ee expect when the Yanks is dealing with a Labour government?' He possibly had a point, it occured to me.

Our near bankruptcy wasn't really an issue. Between the side-tracked diversions, they got round to talking about poor wages in the declining local gloving industry. . . and the need to have a good hour's drinking in the Albion next door before closing time.

My weekly call at the Conservative headquarters at Hendford was pleasant and civilised. It always struck me there was a cruel irony about the old, peeling poster that remained defiantly stuck to one of the inner doors. Churchill looked chubby and avuncular. 'Let him finish the job', it said. Did the constituency committees around the country still want to be reminded of that unavailing election plea – and a nation's rebuff?

The three parties were equally welcoming. They gave me proper cups of tea. They were effusive in their concern for my well-being. They had their paragraphs waiting for me. The only difference between them was in the accent. They all wanted publicity – badly.

All of them seemed to assume that they had my political sympathies. It didn't occur to them that I might even have a contrary point of view. 'Ah, good morning, Matthew. Wasn't that a lovely photograph of Anthony Eden in the *Telegraph*? He's so extraordinarily handsome, isn't he? He'll be such a good prime minister for you and me, won't he?' Or, up over the Unity Hall: 'Too many old men in the Party, haven't we, Matthew? Must weed a few of 'em out. Can't have that two-fingered Churchill back, can we?' I nodded or shook my head in a vague, non-committal way to all of them.

Michael Foot, I was told by the Labour agent, was one of the emerging new stars. Nye was his mentor. 'He even writes for Beaverbrook and knows all about how to put over the message. And he's coming to speak to us.'

The *Gazette* weren't terribly impressed when I told them. 'A stick at the most. That's if there is anything in it.'

I cycled out to Stoke-under-Ham, where the meeting was being held, on a moonlit autumn night – without front or rear light. Traffic irregularities among the cycling fraternity were the norm on the country lanes. There were still relatively few cars on the road. And young PC Carter, the Stoke copper, was something of a friend of the junior reporters. He used to come to the village dances at Coker, a safe distance from his home beat. In Friday night mufti, he impressed those of us familiar with the sight of him reading piously in court from his notebook, when we saw him mooching away in lecherous dalliance over the last waltz. I reckoned that for our silence he owed us a favour or two if our cycle lights weren't working.

It was a packed meeting. This young man breezed in, looking like a last-year university student just off a windswept towpath. He threw off his raincoat and scarf with a mannered offhand flourish. The sports coat and general wardrobe didn't suggest he ever used up his full allocation of thirty-six clothing coupons. Among the elders in the front row, there were approving esoteric looks. He was one of the movement's bright young advocates. They gripped their pint mugs at arm's length. It wasn't time for drinking now.

The style took me by surprise. He began with a few psychological throwaways to woo the main bulk of his audience, mostly men sitting in their pullovers, pulling on their Stars and Woodbines. Soccer was the chummy meeting point. 'Fantastic team you've got in Yeovil – we've all heard about you down in Devon. I love football. Got a season ticket at Home Park, you know.' He pondered on his words. 'That's my only concession to capitalism.' (Laughter.) 'It isn't too big an investment. I don't know how much a season ticket is at Yeovil.'

Impetuously, from my end seat behind the small press table, I shouted back: 'One pound, twelve shillings and sixpence.' I was immediately mortified by my interruption, the only one I was to make during a lengthy and fairly dignified professional life, top heavy in the earlier days with evenings spent listening to lectures, talks and speeches. The fact was I'd just bought a season ticket for a friend and it was information, I felt, worth conveying.

Michael Foot, hair awry and sparse notes screwed up in a clenched, flailing fist, went on for forty-five minutes. Pursuing the soccer theme, he was sorry it had been necessary to postpone all midweek matches for the time being, a move apparently to prevent absenteeism when an economy drive was of urgent importance. He talked warmly of the Beveridge Report, unloved by Churchill; of the fact that trade union membership was going up and that the old order had gone for ever; that although the cupboard was bare at the moment, it wouldn't be for too much longer. There were shafts of Utopian socialism, much to the liking of his devotees. His scorn, when it came to the Conservatives, was uncompromising.

It was breathless, high-pitched, more emotional than intellectual. It had an engaging edge of theatricality. The three reporters had a word with him afterwards. He was quiet, civilised, charming. That also somewhat surprised me after all that thundering idealism.

I wrote a stick and a half (30 lines of 8pt). It still came down to a stick, as ordered. The sub-editor toned it down, put some of the more emotive assertions into dreary indirect speech and made it all read like the contents of a seed catalogue. I was grateful that Mr Foot had by then departed back towards the Tamar.

'Thought you were a bit mean on Michael. I could hardly find the report in the paper,' said the Labour agent when I next saw him. 'Got cut, I'm afraid. All that trouble about the Foot and Mouth disease and the farmers being upset that the army are allowing cross country runs over the land.' It was one of the little lies that local reporters have continually to make to placate the aggrieved.

Suddenly I was finding myself the copy-boy political correspondent. My shorthand was coming along nicely, the main reason I imagine for Mr Chapman to offer that silent, beckoning gesture. 'Do you think you can cycle all the way to Long Sutton on Saturday?' I assured him that my chain was well oiled and that my three speeds were functioning perfectly.

'Right, then. Your biggest job so far. You will be going along to report the speech of a very famous man.' I braced myself for more details. Could it be Winnie himself? A member of the Royal Family? Mr Chapman allowed the sense of onerous responsibility to sink in. His mouth was open, almost impishly, at a contorted angle. 'Mr Harold Macmillan is a very famous man – and is going to be even more famous. Maybe even the prime minister one day. I have that on very good authority.' He delayed for a moment allowing me to speculate on the authority with whom he was supposedly on confidential terms.

'Now he is coming to Long Sutton to speak to all the Conservatives from this division. He will be addressing them at 4.30 sharp. I shall want a well-written report – to go at the top of one of the columns. I shall need three sticks. Three sticks at least, young Matthew. Do you think you can do it?'

The imbalance with poor old (young) Michael didn't strike me at the time. But I saw no great problem in churning out what I imagined would be three hundred words of turgid political platitudes, to go in the paper six days later.

Next morning I went into the Cadena for coffee. Alibis for these beverages and vicarious pleasures were becoming easier as I learned how to embroider my increasing sorties from the office. The rest of the coffee-drinking reporters had left by the time I got there. I found an empty table within Diana's serving territory. She was there, gliding around in those bedroom slippers.

She glanced across and gave a little wave. At a distance of six tables I still blushed. Then she came across to clear the dirty crockery and, with a coquettish movement, to flick the crumbs onto the floor. 'Have the rest of the boys come in yet?' I lied. 'All gone, darling. So I have you all to myself.' It was vintage B-picture dialogue. What was the idea of teasing me like this? I couldn't cope, certainly not as she contrived to bend across me to lay another place on the opposite side of the table. 'Can. . . can I have a coffee, please?'

'Of course.' She saw my discomfort and smiled. 'I'd like a word with you, Matthew, when I come back.' And she was gone, twisting those lovely reptilian hips round the tables and a dozen or so matronly customers, most of whom seemed to be beckoning impatiently for their bill or a second cup of coffee.

I was visibly trembling and it embarrassed me. I hurried to the Gents and combed my hair. What did she want to say to me? I barely knew her. I felt uneasy – and excited – whenever she teased me with a darting look or a saucy farewell. This, I realised with some alarm, was the first time I'd ever been alone with her. I didn't think I could even carry on a coherent conversation.

Back at the table I waited with some dread for her return. Then I spotted her emerging from the kitchen with the tray and one lonely, self-conscious cup of coffee. I pretended I was surprised when she arrived at my table.

'Now then, Matthew, how about it then?'

'How – er – how about. . .what?'

'When are you going to take me out?'

73

I simply couldn't handle this. She was grinning away. The lips were very red and luscious. She had no right to play with me like this. The tray was still in her hand, beautifully balanced.

'Well?'

'Are you. . . serious?'

'Darling, you won't ask me. So I've got to ask for you.'

The affectionate tones of her murmured intimacies made me tingle. Her self-confidence frightened me.

'The cinema,' I said. 'How about the cinema?' It came blurting out. My voice crackled and gurgled and spluttered. It wasn't my voice at all. It was a mixture of panic – and joy.

'Yes, if you like. But I've got a better idea. I'd also like to go with you on one of your jobs.'

This conversation was now rapidly soaring out of my compass. How, for heaven's sake, could I possibly take Yeovil's most vamp-ish waitress on my cemetery calls? Would she wear those bedroom slippers into the rarified inner committee room of the Conservative headquarters?

Did she actually think I had an exciting job? I frantically searched my mind for a looming assignment that might at least appear to invest my role of junior reporter with just the remotest glimmer of glamour. 'I've. . . got to report a big political meeting on Saturday. Harold Macmillan.' Then I remembered: 'But you will be working on Saturday.'

'I'll come with you. I'll go sick if necessary. Where is it?'

'Long Sutton.'

'And what's this chap's name, did you say?'

'Harold Macmillan. They say he could be prime minister one day.'

'I think I've seen a picture of him. He's got a nice moustache. Quite dishy. Yes, I'll come with you.'

I was conscious, just, of the matrons trying to catch her attention. 'I'm holding you up.'

'Yes. But about the flicks, darling. Tonight?'

'At the Gaumont. Starts at half past seven.'

'I'll be there.' And she was gone, leaving me wondering whether it had all been a mythical conversation. But then I realised that both my adolescent head and heart were pounding. I was on the verge of my first date – and with a wordly divorcee the other reporters had said was inaccessible.

She was five or six years older. What did you do on a date like this? What did you talk about? How far did you go? She'd just laugh at me as I spluttered away and tried to string vacuous sentences together. It didn't occur to me for a moment that the idea of teasing and guiding a gauche lad just out of school might excite her. But as I got up from the table I knew I didn't mind being teased. My loins were on fire.

Back in the office after work I spent half an hour in the first-floor lavatory, getting the printer's ink off my hands. These were not the days of deodorants but I stripped down to my old-fashioned vest and lathered in rough, red carbolic under the armpits. I slammed water on my untidy hair and parted it rakishly near the middle, like I'd seen in a Wodehouse illustration. The prewar hair styles, from Coward or cigarette cards, rather appealed to me.

Fame is the Spur was the picture at the Gaumont. It was one I had planned to see, in keeping with my recent political forays. Howard Spring, a friend of the previous parson, had once come to spend a few days at the vicarage in my village. But was his political novel quite right for an opening date? I should have gone for something more frivolous or perhaps more erotic. Rosamund John might be rather too prim and intense for the flighty Diana.

I was waiting outside the cinema at a quarter past seven. I'd checked my parting in the plate-glass window of the fish shop on the corner of Stars Lane. Rather badly, I attempted to affect an aura of small-town sophistication.

And there she was, all of a sudden. She'd stepped off the bus in Middle Street. She wore high heels and the legs were bare. I'd never seen her before without her slippers. The lips were rich crimson, freshly licked I felt to give them a gloss. Her high cheekbones were boldly rouged. Even in the high heels she seemed to glide.

'Hi, darling – hope you haven't been waiting long. Can't rely on these Yeovil buses. But then, you'll be taking me home, won't you?' She giggled, playing with me again.

I didn't even know where she lived but I was ready to spend my twenty-five bob of wages on a taxi fare. As I was feeling, I'd have taken her halfway to London on my crossbar. 'Oh dear, Diana, I'm not sure you'll like the film. I didn't really know what was on.'

'They're all the same to me. We'll still enjoy ourselves.' She giggled again and I couldn't quite see why.

I bought two one-and-ninepennies and Diana led me inside. A torch was beckoning us down one of the aisles. Diana gripped my arm and half-pushed me into the back row. She did it, I sensed, with a practised touch. We moved along towards the centre of the row and the usherette, still flickering her torch, had lost us for ever. I was aware only of a whiff of perfume of the kind that occasionally intoxicated me as pretty, painted girls brushed past in the doorway of a village dancehall. We sank into our cinema seats and at once Diana pressed her legs against mine.

She wriggled and took off her coat. I gave her a furtive glance, out of the corner of my eye, and as I became accustomed to the dim light of the auditorium I could just make out the shape of her nose, the contours of her body. She nestled into me, rubbing a soft chin against my neck. She was very smooth. If the story of Ramsay MacDonald was being loosely enacted on screen, I wasn't seeing any of it.

Buzz had told me weeks ago that you usually put your arm round the girl after five minutes and then systematically began to explore. I knew I just couldn't do anything on my own initiative. 'Please, Diana, please. . . show me how,' I said silently.

I watched the screen with unseeing eyes and unsettled body. My senses were in turmoil. Diana looked towards me, giving me the suggestion of a disarming smile. She took my right arm and placed it round her neck. 'Cuddle me tight, darling – it's what I like,' she whispered. In the same movement, she guided my hand down onto her breast. She gave a little wriggle of approval as if to say, 'There!' My groin was red-hot, aching in a way I'd not experienced before. My hand remained stiff, inhibited. She induced a sensation of fondling by the subtle little twists of her own upper body.

'Please, film, don't end. Go on for ever,' I privately pleaded. But it did eventually end and Diana half turned and brushed my cheek with a kiss. We walked out of the cinema and she gave me a reassuring chuckle. 'That was a nice film, wasn't it, darling?' I nodded; we had both blithely lied. 'You can walk me home. We don't need a taxi. Only about a mile.' She chatted most of the way: animated, bubbly, mock-seductive. Never really telling me a thing about herself. Didn't I realise she'd been making a pass at me for weeks? It was the shy, quiet boys she liked – for a change. Her implication now was that she enjoyed being the teacher.

We held hands, almost primly. I felt I'd known her from child-hood. Here she was, almost motherly, as we strolled in the cool evening air of October towards her home. Back in the cinema with Ramsay MacDonald, her instincts had been obsessively sensual. The dichotomy, mother and mistress, was disquieting and at the same time undeniably arousing.

We got to the end of Gipsy Lane and she said abruptly: 'You'll have to leave me here. But kiss me properly first.' In my impassioned silence, I said: 'Show me, Diana.' She read my expression of uncertainty. She took my hands and led me back against the fencing. Then she eased my body towards her, until my rib cage pressed at her bidding against the firm breasts. She put her mouth to mine. The lips parted and like an eager, curious child I followed. Her lips went on a moist, meandering excursion – and I again followed. I was startled to find her tongue probing deep towards my throat and panicked at first that I was going to choke. Once more I did the same. Her tongue tasted sweet. We stayed adhesively bound for a full minute, no movement now apart from the gentle snaking of two tongues and the swaying of her body against my groin. Sixty seconds at the top of Gipsy Lane was for me a generation of sexual education.

Then she broke away. 'Thank you, darling, we must do it again. You will be more relaxed next time. My life really is a mess. Do you know my boy friend? No, just as well. We'll pretend, you and I, he doesn't exist. And then there's my mother who drinks too much. You must have heard of her – everyone calls her the Black Widow. And, oh yes, a couple more things. I've got Saturday off. When do you want me to be ready to meet this Harry Macmillan?'

'It's Harold. Two o'clock at the War Memorial. And what was the other thing?'

'Thought you might like to know. I had an operation when I was married. Can't have a baby. Yes, thought you'd like to know.'

One sentence, one disjointed after another, in that husky, breathless voice. All too much for me to absorb, though not that final nuance.

I pulled out my brown pinstripe for the Saturday. The prospect of what my dream-tart might wear for the meeting of the divisional association of the Tory Party filled me with apprehension.

She was already there, by the War Memorial. She looked rather like some of the Windmill girls in those sexy outdoor publicity shots. The make-up was bold; there was arguably one button more than necessary undone on the turquoise blouse. She was making male heads turn. Expensive silk stockings covered her legs. How many American officers had she – or her mother – known? If she looked a trifle more courtesan than county girl, I wasn't complaining. I was a sixteen-year-old currently more preoccupied with the thought of blissful probing tongues than my imminent appointment with Mr Macmillan.

We went on the bus to Long Sutton, although I wasn't at all sure I'd be able to claim back my fare after telling Mr Chapman I would be going on my bike. Diana and I sat close together, our legs touching. Her presence created more than passing interest. Passengers were turning round to look. Most of the women still had the functional asexual appearance of the war years. Their colours were drab; the clothing hung shapelessly on most of them. In the country districts, they didn't bother much with their make-up. To them, Diana must have appeared a bit too much like an attractive young ostentatious whore, back in the province on holiday. They didn't quite know how anyone could dress as brazenly as that on the rattling green National to Long Sutton. And who was that callow youth sitting self-consciously at her side? She returned their looks, the red lips parted in arrogant challenge.

As we neared the well-heeled Ham-stone village, she turned to me. 'I won't let you down.' I felt I should have been saying it to her.

We had no difficulty finding the big field where the autumn fayre was taking place. A woman with the face of an ageing point-to-pointer was on the gate taking the shilling admissions. 'From the *Gazette*,' I said grandly and she waved us through. Diana was impressed, I could see. We had got there with time to spare. So we had a go on the treasure-hunt and I skittled for a pig. I knocked down seven pins. The farmer, who had taken my sixpence, said: 'Bad luck, son. Only just missed the landlord.' The sticker-up, in his shirtsleeves, rolled back the skittles. 'I'll get back to do the milkin' now, boss. See you later on.' Sticking-up was an occasional therapy he enjoyed. It was usually worth five bob at the end of the night.

They found a lad to take over and I paid sixpence for Diana. She put two skittles off the improvised alley and scattered a little group of idle observers. 'Got to do a bit better than that, miss.' Everyone laughed. Something told me my dream-tart hadn't been so happy for a long time.

At four o'clock I went in search of the Tory officials. I found them with their big blue rosettes and their solid tweeds. 'Has Mr Macmillan arrived yet, please? I'm from the *Gazette*. We've been invited to report the speech.'

The hard-eyed secretary was peering suspiciously at my companion. It wasn't the most hospitable of scrutinies. Diana had presence but perhaps not class. In the intuitive ways of a middle-class woman, the secretary could also see Diana as too much of a distraction among the sherry glasses which I could just spy laid out for committee and VIPs on a trestle table inside the marquee. 'This. . . is my friend. She's very keen to hear Mr Macmillan.'

'Oh dear, now that's a pity. We have just the one place for the press in the front row. Maybe your – er – friend wouldn't mind standing at the back.'

As a boy not long out of school, nurtured in rural ways, I was hardly well versed in social etiquette. But I felt that a slight was being perpetrated. I became consumed with a hitherto unknown surge of gallantry. 'Well – em – no, I don't think that would be quite right. We'd like to be together. I'll stand at the back as well.' This produced an awkward silence and I produced a daring card. 'I'll do my best to hear. But you will have to forgive me if I don't get it all quite right.'

The secretary left us abruptly. She flounced back towards the marquee entrance and was soon in tetchy, intense conversation with a male member of the committee. He looked in our direction. He lingered over Diana. Their eyes met; he nodded to her in an almost guilty fashion and they exchanged smiles. The conversation with the secretary went on. Then she returned.

'We have had a word about it. And we think we can perhaps squeeze in one more place in the middle of the front row. It isn't going to be easy.' She didn't need to add that; it was implicit in her frigid voice.

Everyone, or at least everyone with a big blue rosette, started moving into the marquee. The enthusiasm was even more muted. 'You had better come in with the rest of us. We are going to have a glass of sherry with our special guest before he delivers his speech.'

Diana darted a look at me. She took my hand again and squeezed it. She looked quite strikingly flash, she looked adorable and, for one fleeting moment, she looked very vulnerable. If I had possessed more confidence myself, I'd have hugged her and led her forward with an assertive step. She recovered and assumed once more that untutored, rather brash poise.

We walked into the big tent together and joined a long line for the introductions. The sherry was offered us off a silver salver. It was sweet, good quality. Diana drank it with eager gulps, fast as I emptied a Cadena coffee cup on one of the mornings I was on stolen time. She ran her tongue along her lips to savour the final taste. I wanted to see her do it again.

There were so many snatches of sycophantic small-talk that it took a long time for us to reach the head of the queue. A constituency official, briefed by the displeased secretary, said to Mr Macmillan: 'This is a young fellow from. . . the local weekly newspaper. A very good paper, too, sir. He is keen to report your speech. Will that be in order?'

I wanted to say: 'Hang on, you pompous so-and-so. You invited us here and your association is after the publicity. I could have been watching Stocky leading out Yeovil Town or playing right half for the opposition' (League of Youth).

The Member for Bromley put out his hand. There was a caricaturist's droop to the moustache but he was still a formidable and handsome figure. He really was an amalgam of Eton, Balliol, the Guards and the Athenaeum. He seemed to be enjoying the adulation of the party workers, dispensing the pleasantries in a languidly attractive voice. He was wearing an impeccable Savile Row suit, a blue handkerchief protruding from the breast pocket. There were more women than men pressing forward to meet him.

'And this must be your – your young lady. Charming gel. Yes, charming.'

Diana possessed an innate eloquence without needing to speak. She compressed a whole evening of innuendoes into an almost coy smile. He was still absorbing himself in this tangible communication of silence as he was being introduced to the next couple.

The speech, when it came, was as thespian as it was political. He measured his pauses, caressed and elongated his carefully fashioned phrases. He turned to every corner of his audience; each party follower felt he was talking specially to them. I had heard Wolfit and Donat on the wireless, and now thought of them both. In that slightly weary country-squire manner, he transfixed his disciples. He wasn't averse to stirring alliteration and a poetic, rehearsed afterthought. Some of his ideas were a good deal more liberal in concept than the regional faithful were used to. But he was an adept performer. He never went too far. There was enough traditional Conservatism to placate the momentarily startled members of his flock. He extolled the way the Somerset farmers had kept tilling the land during the war; one could detect the murmurs of approval all around. At the end there was prolonged applause. Mac beamed and gave a theatrical bow. He was much loved.

Diana and I were sitting between the divisional chairman and a person I assumed was Mac's agent. I took down my shorthand notes with professional aplomb. Diana watched me with increasing admiration; once or twice she jerked my arm playfully. For most of the time she watched the speaker.

On the bus, going back to Yeovil, she said to me: 'Didn't he talk well. I think I could vote Conservative, you know. A snooty lot, though. Did you see that committee chap in the blue suit? Made a pass at me. Silly little twat!' Mock scorn one moment, a little slip in dignity the next.

I didn't like to hear about that smarmy little official in the blue suit. I suppose I was jealous, something I had never experienced before. It wasn't what you expected at a Tory rally, among the tweeds and the polished voices.

We snuggled up in the rear seat of the nearly empty National. 'Bit of a thrill that for me. Just to go to something like that. Will you take me with you again, to something else?'

'I'd like to.' How about tomorrow, and the next day, I wanted to say.

'Just occasionally it may have to be. I've got a complicated life.' She clearly had no intention at all of telling me how complicated.

She had chatted that afternoon with Harold Macmillan and been called a charming gel. I felt he took more interest in her than all those committee women and their friends who swooned as they squeezed his hand and gushed their inane flatteries. Mac was a famous man, according to Mr Chapman, and he wasn't the least concerned that she spent most of the week serving Cadena coffee and riding the insults of dissatisfied customers. I knew then I'd be proud to take her anywhere.

We had got to the end of Gipsy Lane and she broke in on my reverie of inordinate pride over her new, emerging status.

'Will you be doing the court on Tuesday? My mum is up. Cider this time. She got home and pulled the canary's neck out.'

SIX

The Big Freeze

HAST THEE TRIED these hure snoek, then? – dussin know wus comin' next.'

'Dried bloody eggs from America, now snoek. Whatever that is. No taste to it, I'll tell 'ee. 'Taint fish as I do know it.'

I'd propped by bike against Mr Moger's village stores and was waiting my turn. Just half a dozen candles for my mother. She had said she needed them to build up her reserve for what was going to be a long, hard winter. Mum and Dad could always tell what the weather would be like in the months ahead. They didn't look at *Old Moore's* for that kind of information. They just gazed around at nature – and they knew.

'Bloody snoek. Do 'ee see they'm changin' the name back to barracuda. Sound a bit better – but same taste. Wo's thee got fer us to eat, Bob?'

Mr Moger, eyes habitually crafty as a ferret's and craggy face that remained unaltered through the changing seasons, pointed to a couple of seed boxes lined up in the window. Spread out across them were half a dozen rooks. 'There 'tis! Rook pie. Killed 'em meself, through the brain – not riddled wi' shot. And they'm fresh.'

I looked at the raddled old birds, with their bloodied heads and contorted eyes, and was unconvinced. I may have imagined it but I thought they carried the tang of long dead flesh. A scraggy tortoise-shell cat snuggled against the seed boxes, in no visible way impressed by the proximity of Bob's gastronomic delicacy. 'Nothing like a rook pie,' he said. It seemed a reasonable statement, even though his fer-rety eyes reflected an enthusiasm not requited.

When it was my turn, I bought a quarter of brown mints and ordered the candles. 'Not many to spare, son. Everybody's getting they things in fer the winter. Goin' to be a cold 'un, lad.' They were clearly unanimous about that.

I liked Old Bob. He took a passing interest in my status as a budding reporter around the local villages. 'Take you out wi' me one day when I'm shootin' them rooks. I be the best shot fer miles. You could write a nice little tale about that.'

'Never tasted a rook, Mr Moger. Are they better than pigeons?'

He spread his gnarled hands as if I shouldn't reveal such ignorance when it came to the family table. 'The missus do do 'em in rough cider. And lovely bit of meat off the breast.' I shot a stealthy glance back into the window. As far as I could see, there wasn't much meat anywhere.

Bob changed the subject. 'The passon was in hure just now. He's 'specking a big lot in church for armistice service, Sunday after next. Legion think they got the best turnout yet. You also ought to write summit about that.'

Until then I hadn't really thought of Old Bob as either an especially devoted man of God or eager advocate for the British Legion. Maybe they placed a sizeable order for rook pies when it came to the Legion's annual supper.

A few days later I suggested to the *Gazette* that I should cover the service. 'Just a line or two, if you like. We'll be doing half a column on the armistice parade in Yeovil – but we could tack a paragraph of yours on at the end. See if the vicar has anything to say about the state of the nation. And don't forget to give the name of the bugler.' Names. . . names. Yet maybe in this case it genuinely reflected interest in brass band music, on the part of one normally insensitive sub.

There were forty-three members of the local branch of the British Legion who grouped up outside the headquarters, a quarter of a mile from the church. Some of them had pinned their medals to their faded lapels; some were in their demob suits. Almost all looked hollow-cheeked and serious. They lined up in three ranks with a minimum of formality. No question of shortest-on-the-left, tallest-on-the-right. Officers lined up with privates, of which there were many more. 'By the left, quick march!' ordered someone with a quiet, self-conscious voice. It was almost as if he had forgotten what he used to say. And they moved off, all of them instinctively in step, standard-bearer at the head. They didn't swing their arms high but the old drill-square discipline had not deserted them. They were all of a sudden consumed with patriotism and sad memories. The rest of us walked behind them, equally serious and contemplative.

In the church the flag was lowered with reverence and the names of twenty-eight men from the parish, who had lost their lives in the two world wars, were slowly read out. . .'AB Albert Ackerman, RN Division; Gunner John Baker, RM Artillery; Private John Boucher, Grenadier Guards; Private Henry Farnham, Dorset Regiment; Captain Howard Helyar, Rifle Battalion; Lance-Sergeant Walter English, Somerset Light Infantry. . .'

A one-armed bugler from Hardington blew the Last Post. The vicar paid his tribute from the pulpit. I saw Mrs Thompson, who had lost her only son and breadwinner, Ronnie, crying during the service. Then the forty-three men from the Legion, proud, brave, mostly ordinary men, marched back down the hill, past the Tudor almshouses. It was very moving. 'Legion branch, dismiss!' They did a little right turn and almost in the same movement pulled out their Woodbines.

'Tell you what, Arthur. Couldn't order arms now to save me life.'

'Don't think we'll ever have to again. Once were quite enough.'

I also saw the officers talking to the privates. They were using Christian names, hesitantly, not quite naturally. But it was a start. The accents were different, though the friendship in the voice appeared real enough. It made me feel that Coker had changed in the last seven or eight years.

The parish's social divisions, created by the accident of birth, had always bothered me. Now I sensed a mighty movement, in conjunction with the radical, exciting, unsettling words of Attlee, Morrison and Bevan. There was much talk I didn't understand about workers' control. The coal industry, the railways, electricity and gas were being nationalised. There was talk next of iron and steel. A free National Health Service would be operating over the next eighteen months.

These were the reforms promised to the soldiers if they voted Labour in. Most boys of my age were carried along by the romance of a blanket political philosophy we hadn't seen at close quarters before. We heard the voluminous qualms of the City boardrooms and decided there was too much self-interest involved. 'We must get these Socialists out before they ruin the country for ever and turn it into another Russia,' was a recurrent plea which intrigued rather than troubled me.

Village lads like me, not so long out of school and with a risible knowledge of economics, imagined everything would be transformed in an air of political romance, without a hitch. We left it to politicians we instinctively warmed to. Why should we be expected to know anything about the Dollar Gap, international antagonisms and an appallingly fragile financial foundation upon which it was virtually impossible to carry through sweeping changes with hope of instant success?

And why should I – Matt Fouracre, frustrated cub reporter whose simple aspirations didn't really extend far beyond a weekly byline, a pretty girl to walk home after a Saturday dance or maybe even a hat trick for the local team – be expected to know that political ideals took into account everything but erratic and selfish whims of human nature?

When I saw the wizened ex-officer from the First World War talking to the Coker twine worker, a private in the Pay Corps during the Second World War – after the armistice parade – I accepted without question that it was part of a widespread social change.

Conveniently I tried to forget that this former officer had sat on the top table at our cricket club's annual supper a month before and snorted with indignation when he saw one of these same villagers, now members of the Legion, start to smoke before the loyal toast.

'My God, look at that!' he had said. 'Hasn't anyone told him? Such damned discourtesy.'

It wasn't discourtesy, I'd wanted to say. And no-one had ever told him differently. He was smoking because that was what he always did at home after a meal. It was his way of relaxing in the conviviality of the cricket club supper he had earned after being away for six years. And I didn't think the King would object.

The Legion flagstaff was folded down and put back in its case. Coker's ex-soldiers and sailors remained strangely serious.

'Sometimes I do wonder who won the war. Shortages everywhere. Empty bloody larders. Rationing. They didn't tell us it were going to be like this.'

'All we want now is a freeze-up. Never get through the winter, we wouldn't.'

'Still living with thee in-laws, Ken?'

'Yeh, and can't stand it much longer. Three kids now – and the missus. Shouting and bawling all the time. But what chance have we got of getting on the housing list? Me and me brother is going to try to get our families into one of they Nissen huts where the balloons was.'

'Squatting' was a new word. Rather reluctantly the editor had agreed to use it in headlines. People in the office thought it sounded too much like a slang term. In fact, it meant social necessity.

Every week there were stories in the papers, including the *Gazette*, about the way families, desperate for somewhere to live, were taking over disused army and RAF camps, barrage balloon sites and other derelict buildings on wasteland. They were simply arriving with their pathetic sticks of furniture and moving in. It wasn't exactly legal but the local authorities and the police were inclined to pretend it wasn't happening.

The country was embarrassingly short of homes. Those prefabs were one inadequate sop. Many thousands of houses had been lost in the bombing. Now all the servicemen had also come back from the war. A great many of them were getting married. Repressed passions were unleashed and the birthrate was soaring. The Government was hopelessly behind with its rebuilding programme. It was in no mood for encouraging private development. And all the time the Board of Trade was bickering with the Ministry of Works, in bureaucratic high dudgeon over almost everything – bricks, cement, paint and timber.

Reports came into the *Gazette* office every day of a new lot of squatters moving in. There was much huffing and puffing from parish councillors and intransigent neighbours. Some of the letters were unsigned. Most of them made the same point, more or less: 'This is worse than the gipsies.'

I was given the job of collating all the reports about the squatters. I put them into some kind of order, influenced by my idea of human interest. The reports were pinned together and each Wednesday afternoon were handed over to a sub-editor, for him to turn them into a column of copy. It didn't take me long to discover that my news judgment varied sharply from his. 'Anarchy' was a strong word and he used it in several of his headlines. An irate reader had written in to protest about groups of squatters 'taking the law into their own hands in what is nothing less than anarchy.'

At the time I wasn't absolutely sure what the word meant. I felt it had something to do with political subversives planting homemade bombs in the pursuit of the overthrow of plutocracy. I'd read about anarchists once in a short story by Jack London. They weren't anything to do with disillusioned ex-servicemen desperate for a bare room to put down a frayed mattress for their wives and children.

The national papers told me that as many as 20,000 homeless people were now 'squatting' in any form of disused military building they could find. The *Daily Mirror*, which I read with a fervent admiration then for its simple, well-written journalism aimed at ordinary people, was predictably sympathetic to the squatters. *The Times* and *Telegraph* seemed rather less so. The *Daily Worker* wasn't taken at the *Gazette* but I used to snatch a stealthy glance at it in the public Reading Room, where it staked its democratic claims; it became almost orgasmic with delight when it reported that a group of homeless ex-servicemen, back from fighting in the same campaign as the Russians, had actually dared to take over Duchess of Bedford House in opulent Kensington. I preferred the account of how some squatters, as opportunistic as desperate, had installed themselves in the better decorated quarters of an RAF station while the officers were at a camp dance.

Squatting was fast becoming a national neurosis. There was much compassion for the cause within the *Gazette* office, especially the reporters' room. We were more or less the same age. We wore our consciences with conspicuous pride. Don, not long out of the army himself, said: 'Good luck to the poor sods – we ought to do a leader about it.' But my dear old weekly paper was inclined to recoil from such emotional issues. There was a danger, in taking sides, of conflicting with the *Gazette's* traditional establishment stance, maybe it was thought.

Every day we heard of a new takeover. In Bristol it was Bedminster Down and the golf course at Shirehampton. At Taunton it was Burnshill Camp. Dozens moved into an unoccupied military base at Cricket St Thomas and around the Chard area, previously used by the American troops. There were 'great treks of homeless families' to South Somerset.

At Chard, the Rural Council didn't really know what to do. There were problems over water supplies and hygiene. Whole committee meetings were devoted to the vexed topic. A typed message was sent to the local squatters. 'We regret to inform you that it is not possible to provide sufficient facilities to make the huts reasonably habitable and we recommend you to move as quickly as possible.'

'Get stuffed!' was the militant response. And by thirteen votes to twelve, the council finally agreed to transport water to the huts for one month.

On my own initiative, I cycled one lunch hour to where I knew some Nissen huts left over from a balloon site were being occupied. The site was at the back of Summerleaze Park School, near to some pleasant suburban houses. In my pocket was a copy of one of the letters sent to my paper. It was from an angry local resident, complaining about the insanitary conditions and the danger to others' health. I could see a story here.

All the peeling, run-down huts were now occupied. Young house-wives, in their pinnies, lank hair thrust back under their scarves, were chatting animatedly one to the other. They didn't appear to be stopping for any sign of a lunchbreak. They were brushing, scrubbing, dusting. They were beating doormats against the outside walls. Those ugly huts were already spotless, treated as if they were marble palaces. The housewives' joy and enthusiasm, and sense of sheer relief, were unbridled. It was their first home.

One of them, savouring the enterprise of her husband, had pinned a big notice on the door: THIS ONE IS TAKEN. This was their territory, their very own. There was in their mood a mixture of defiance, euphoria, good humour. A noisy, joyful fellow-feeling pervaded the old balloon site, overgrown though it was with brack-en and thick, coarse grass wilting in the winds of early winter. They invited me to look inside the huts. Improvised curtains were hanging in the windows. Family snaps were carefully arranged on the tops of the chest-of-drawers; many of the photographs were of servicemen in uniform. Most of the huts had babies in cots, whimpering contentedly as if aware of a new found family freedom.

'The nipper could eat off the floor. I've swept all the muck out. Soon be like a real house. Hubby's gone to a sale to pick up a bit more furniture.'

'But what about the water?'

'We're waiting for the council to do something. And we can always use the public lav down the road. We aren't complaining.'

I pointed out that some of the local residents were.

'Listen, Eric my hubby was six years in the Navy. U-boats and all that. Didn't think I'd ever see him again. Surely the country owe him something or other in return. Say just four walls to be going on with. And them!', she broke off to point to some of the neat little suburban homes nearby. 'I bet half of them was army-dodgers. Getting fat while Eric was nearly getting sunk.'

It was an illogical, understandable form of prejudice that persisted for some years after the war.

I checked how much of my lunch hour was left and hur-ried along to one of those houses. The number on the freshly painted brown gate coincided with the one on the letter in my pocket. A man in his sixties opened the door, no more than halfway.

'We try to keep the draught out when winter comes. . .'

'I'm from the *Gazette*. We're thinking about doing something on the squatters,' I fibbed, head turning towards the direction of the Nissen huts.

'And I should think so, too. Disgraceful. Soon we'll be overrun with vermin, as they throw out their rubbish. You can see what kind of people they are. No furniture. Babies everywhere. Sleep on the floor, I imagine. I've written to your editor about it, you know.'

'Well yes, but I wondered if there was anything else you wanted to say. You must feel very strongly.'

Much of my journalistic apprenticeship to date had been self-taught. But I knew there were times when you had to smarm and imply that the person you were interviewing had all your sympathy.

'You can see for yourself. If we're not careful, this place is going downhill fast. I bought it for my wife and myself just before the war. We pay the rates, you know. And one day we may want to sell. What chance would we have with that lot down there. They've got no regard for the law. Where will it end?'

The *Gazette*, whatever its faults in those days, was still renowned, at least in its news columns, for its sense of balance. I felt I must put the other point of view, even if the argument of a raw, spotty teenager was apt to lack weight. 'They seem to be cleaning the place up – and some of the huts are looking quite nice inside.'

'You'd say different to that if you lived next door to them.'

I thought about what one of the housewives had said about army-dodgers and decided it was worth an oblique probe. Tact was needed.

'I – er – expect you were in the army. . .First World War. . .It must be hard coming back, of course, with nowhere to live.'

'No, I wasn't in the Services. Both times I was in a reserved occupation. But I did my bit, I can tell you. Air-raid warden, fire-watching. Things like that. We tried to preserve the old town and keep it ticking over for when the boys came back.'

I went back to the office and typed out my story. Reluctantly, I kept away from the army-dodging innuendoes. My piece began: 'Angry squatters at a former barrage balloon site in Yeovil last night confronted local residents who want them moved on. . .'

I wrote it from the squatters' point of view. It was they who were 'angry'. My ten paragraphs added up to a biased, immature piece of reportage, revealing without any doubt at all where my emotions lay. All my squatters were war heroes. Their wives were clean, industrious and motherly. They were always 'hugging their four-month-old baby' as they made their articulate points. By comparison, my local residents were by implication uncaring and snooty.

My story was handed in with the remainder of the squatter reports and I heard no more about it. On the Thursday, tortured by curiosity and more than a modicum of vanity, I searched through the proofs. As I was doubtless providing the main lead for the week's round-up, I fantasized over the prospect of a 'By M.F.' at the top of the column. The Summerleaze wives were going to be very happy. . . 'Some young chap from the local paper came to see us. About time someone gave our side of the argument. . .'

I eventually found my contribution. There were fourteen lines, almost at the end of the round-up. There was a brief quote from one of the wives, a slightly longer one from the man I'd spoken to. No names were given. The quotes were bland to the point of being meaningless.

The sub-editor concerned called me over on the Friday morning. 'Did you see your piece, there with the rest? Couldn't quite use it like you wrote it – not our style, is it? Had to cut it, of course, but I used a bit of both sides.' He paused: 'Showed it to Cherry. He didn't think we should get too involved. All a bit delicate with the Council at the moment.'

I felt like charging straight out and applying for a job with the *Evening World*. It was the start of a miserable winter.

First there was Foot and Mouth. Thousands of cattle had to be destroyed. The strain in Dorset and Somerset was said to be 'particularly virulent'. One of our district reporters broke free of the strictures of the *Gazette* style-book and sent in a marvellous eye-witness account of how an old farmer sobbed uncontrollably when his whole stock was lost for ever. 'What's Sam playing at?' was the office reaction. 'Can't he stick to the facts? Farmers don't cry.'

Well, I knew better than that. A few weeks earlier I had sat in on a court case in which a farmer was found guilty of adding water to his milk supply. He sat in the dock and for a full minute, his body heaved as he sobbed. I was never quite sure whether it was because he'd been found out – or because he had to part with fifty quid.

After Foot and Mouth came the floods, all across the country. I could imagine what it was like when the sea came all the way from the Bristol Channel to Glastonbury. The *Gazette* carried a story about the Vicar of Mudford getting marooned and having to cancel Sunday services. It wasn't the slightly satirical and irreverent version that Buzz had offered.

I set off to work in my wellingtons. Dad was a worrier. 'Be careful going through the water – the brakes will pack up on the bike. Never be safe for you going down Hendford Hill.'

That wasn't the problem. It was the flooding round Halves Lane and the roadway alongside the Saw Mills. The water was up to thirty inches. I put my cycle on my shoulder, climbed through a gap in the hedge and began squelching my way along the elevated grass for two hundred yards.

I looked down at the road. The baker's van hadn't made it. Reg, the driver, was still seated in the cab. He was pulling on his pipe with an expression of resignation. It struck me that he'd never starve to death – not with those cottage loaves in the back. He saw me and wound down his window. 'Just as well have a pipe of baccy. Better than trying to work out them damn rationing regulations every house I call at – it's a bugger, I'm telling you.' He surveyed his own plight, the stranded van. 'And so is this!'

Reg was a born pessimist. 'You won't never get to Yeovil. Might as well go home and save the furniture instead. The whole of Somerset's under water. The Yeo. . . the Parrett. . . the Tone. . . they'm all overflowin'.'

'What are you going to do? Can I help, Reg?'

'Just biding hure till someone comes and hauls me out. They've phoned, over at the Saw Mills.' He relit his pipe.

I got to the office two hours late. I was always adept at finding excuses but today's was genuine enough. It still needed embroidery. 'Terrible floods everywhere in Coker. Worst in living memory.'

'Give me a few pars about it, then,' said Don, who'd been assigned to do the local flooding story. He knew of my tendency towards exaggeration. 'But just give us the facts. . . more or less.'

I did, more or less. East Coker's readers must still have been surprised to discover, when they opened their papers on the Friday morning, that the village had been virtually cut off for several days. Vital bread and other food supplies had never got through. There were instances of hardship and a flu epidemic was beginning to rage. The doctor from West Coker had been forced back by the unprecedented floods in Halves Lane. A baby prematurely born at Tellis Cross had been delivered by a neighbour. It seemed to devalue the story, I had reasoned, to mention that the neighbour was a qualified midwife.

Coker took its place, in the paper, with the worst hit villages of the West Country. There was sympathy from outside, frowns from inside. No-one wrote to the editor to question journalistic licence.

Instead, the parish was inclined to bask in its new found importance alongside the nation's disaster areas. Over the months that followed, outsiders would say: 'Awful time you had in your village during the floods. We read all about it. We all felt for you. Oh dear, we do hope you've dried out by now.'

'Just about,' they would be told. The fact was that by now everyone in the parish really did believe it all – the worst floods in living memory, lack of food and a flu epidemic.

After the floods, real or imagined, there was the cruel, biting cold. It arrived a week or so before Christmas. The paraffin lamp still burned – on the kitchen table at home – but there were electricity failures all over town.

Shopping had to be done by candlelight. As a cosy Christmas-card image it might sound apposite. In reality it brought only confusion and short tempers. Harassed shopkeepers searched vainly in the gloom for their modest merchandise before picking their way back towards the till. Avarice, impatience and a catastrophic power system made up an unattractive mixture.

The roads were far too treacherous for me to cycle to work. I got a lift one or two mornings from a local solicitor and walked the four miles home at night. One evening I left work ten minutes early and bought mother a tea trolley for a Christmas present. It wasn't heavy but was an awkward piece of furniture to carry, especially over four miles. The easiest way, I found, was to steady it horizontally on my head. I was reminded of pictures I'd seen of old Greek peasant women carrying sacks of grain home to make bread.

It was a slow, rather comic, journey for me, only lightened when Mr Vowles caught up with me and pulled on the reins. I was helped up onto the wagon. My tea trolley, loosely encased in brown paper, was heaved onto the back to be bedded into the remnants of the farmyard manure. The old carthorse, freshly shod and now uncertain of its step on the icy road, clattered forward. Mother was profuse in her thanks. It was her first tea trolley and it was immediately put into the front room, next to the sofa. If she thought the dark wood had a distinctive smell, she said nothing.

The Christmas of 1946 lacked joy. Even the pubs had a chilly aura of gloom. The streets were as dark as they'd been during the blackout. 'Shiver with Shinwell' said the headlines. We all felt we deserved better than this after the war. Only the black market was thriving. Some of the girls showed off their seamless nylon stockings, oblivious to the fact that they'd been bought by their boy friends off the spivs. We used to see the spivs in Yeovil, all of them dressed just like Arthur English, in their long, wide, gaudy ties.

At least we'd had cosy make-the-best-of-it Christmases during the war, when we killed the tough old Rhode Island rooster and defiantly put up the trimmings. The Christmas of 1946 was a miserable anti-climax. There was no heating in the churches. We huddled in our overcoats and the words of the carols froze on our lips.

The cold eased for a few weeks and the snow thawed. I didn't need, any longer, to go to work with Dad's spade tied to the crossbar. We all began to grin again and do our traditional, rather smug, imitation of British survival valour. Then suddenly that alien winter, far more vicious and fearsome this time, returned. It took us by surprise. We'd swept the snow away once and were even talking of snowdrops.

Now the wind was howling in unabated belligerence again, bringing down the trees and blocking the roads. And then came the snow once more, swirling in blind fury all across the West Country. There was an ominous sprinkling when we went to bed. In the morning it was four feet high: and still more on the way. No question of getting to work – I struggled no farther than my front gate.

Instead I helped Dad dig a token track through the drifts. He had his priorities right. The rough-hewn pathway led from the front door to the top of the garden, where our lean-to lavatory had been given a little protection by a spreading yew tree which we always felt was as old as the parish church. 'No damn sense digging a way down to the gate,' said Dad. 'We won't have any roundsmen getting even halfway up Hendford Hill.' The trackway to the lavatory carried a more practical logic altogether.

We had a two-seater in the style of many of the country cottages. In truth I never shared my excretions with anyone but the crude double-facility must have had its uses. 'Just right if you've bin eatin' prunes and can't hang on any longer. Then 'tis hell fer leather and two at a time!' we'd say with an earthy unself-conscious humour.

I hated going to our privy. It was bad enough in the summer months when you sat, tense and helplessly exposed, listening to the bumble bees and the dung flies buzzing around in the dark, inches from your bottom. In the winter, you simply shivered. It was necessary to carry a torch in the evenings and you saw the goose pimples on your bare upper legs. 'Do your business and come back in the warm as soon as you can,' Mum used to say. As a boy, I was tempted to pray for eternal constipation during the bitter winter months.

During that awful 1947, when I was stranded at home, I couldn't even send a phoned message to the office from the New Inn across the road. The phone was out of use – most of them were. My parents and I sipped hot Oxo and listened to the wireless, crackling more than ever, in the bleak, windy atmosphere.

It was all so depressing. We kept hearing the clipped sentences of Cripps, schoolmasterly, without emotion, telling us how serious everything was. Absolute priority, when it came to coal, would have to be given to the electricity stations. Industry couldn't expect any more than half its usual quota of solid fuel. And warnings seemed to get worse by the bulletin. On the West Region news, from Bristol, we were told of dislocated transport, blocked roads and hardship. In the towns, where snow ploughs were gradually making it possible to get around, the doctors' surgeries were full. There was grave loss of livestock on many isolated farms on Dartmoor and Exmoor. 'And nearer home,' said my grandfather. 'Just think of them poor little sheep huddling together and freezing to death even up in the park hure.'

The bulletins advised us to keep warm. We were clearly a nation of aches, pains and coughs. There was nothing much to do, imprisoned in our dark little cottage. I stood by the window and scrutinised every page, every 'ad', from the last week's *Gazette*. On the front page was a big advert for Fynnon Salts, especially for rheumatism sufferers: 'Large size 1s 6d (including purchase tax).' For two fewer pence, we could buy pick-me-up Yeast Vite tablets. Everyone needed a tonic, it implied. You could say that again. Then I looked at what would have been on offer at the Gaumont, if only the cinema could have been open to the public. Johnny Weissmuller in *Tarzan Escapes*. The advert showed his bare, rippling, well-fed torso. It made me resentful. Many of us were guilty of that simmering envy, something left over from the war. And here was a Yank, I was illogically saying, who didn't know what it was like to be cold.

Miraculously after two or three days, the postman got through on foot. No-one quite knew how he managed it. He delivered a few letters and cleared the box, putting the contents into a second sack he had slung over his shoulder. We gave him hot drinks and he told us what things were like in Yeovil, where the glove factories had closed and no-one was going into the handful of shops which had stayed open. He waited while I wrote a letter to my editor, apologising that I couldn't get into the office but that somehow or other, I'd be there on Thursday. And I was. We worked by candlelight when it began to get dark. I wrote graphically about a stranded village. It was becoming a habit.

The dear, old *Gazette* may have often been dull, tradition-bound, unadventurous. But it was a trouper in times of crisis. The front doors of the office, up the dangerous, snow-impacted steps, were kept open. The commercial department hatch remained ajar in optimistic invitation to those who contemplated trudging in with their small ads.

There were paraffin lamps everywhere, and dripping candles stuck in the Dickensian inkwells. Up in the composing room, one heard the intermittent moans and near-panic as yet another power cut caused the metal pots on the linotype machines to get cold and lead to more delays. But, almost miraculously, the presses still rolled on the Thursday. The edition schedules had to be drastically revised and in many cases telescoped with scant regard for geographical bounds. There was much patient waiting for power supplies to be restored – and schoolboyish cheers when they were. The papers came off the presses, defiant if not 'hot' in the popular sense. Then came the distribution problems. Some of the vans were already abandoned with frozen radiators; some of the regular drivers were still stranded a long way from Yeovil. Private cars were ingeniously conjured up, greatcoats still strapped crudely across the bonnets for added engine warmth, and chains fastened to the wheels. Papers were bundled in and, if the trains were running again, transported to the local stations.

For ten days I walked to work, adeptly stepping in the tracks of others or taking advantage of the indentations caused by farm wagons. My father, fearful of further falls of snow, insisted that I carry a spade. I made a ludicrous sight. My mother each morning pushed a torch into my thick overcoat pocket, followed by a tin of Zubes. It was, I suppose, a sort of survival kit. 'If you get stuck, knock on the nearest door – people die in the snow.' I knew how Captain Scott must have felt.

Once I reached the top of Hendford Hill the conditions were better. Old Austins were now rattling along, at a crawl, on their chains. But there were no buses. Everyone was walking to work, in twos and threes. My world was white, cold and unreal. We affected conviviality through chattering teeth and set expressions.

'They Ruskies is used to it – they'm hardy buggers.' There was still a strong affection for the Russian soldiers for the way they helped to sway the pendulum of war. We were not quite sure how to apportion their contribution and were uneasy about their initial allegiance to the other side. But we knew, whatever the turncoat politics, that they had in the end stopped Hitler in his tracks. And all of us seemed to agree, in the context of early-morning conversation on Hendford Hill, that the Ruskies were 'hardy buggers' when it came to the weather.

There was no end to the dire warnings from the Government over those ghastly winter months. The acute shortage of coal brought a resourceful response from Dad. He organised the three of us to walk, over the next three Saturdays – all sport was cancelled so I was free – up across the park to Spin Wood. Dad carried a small chopper with him. We industriously gathered dead wood which my father tied into faggots, one for each of us. He kept the heaviest for himself. Mum and I both slung our faggots onto our shoulders and we all trudged back, down to the village. We left the wood to dry in front of the fire for a few days.

The bulletins on the wireless were laden with news of increasing restrictions and pleas for domestic economy. Industry in many parts of the country was now without electricity. Gas had been drastically cut. I sat with my grandfather and heard Attlee give the very first political broadcast. We listened intently, in the way we listened to Churchill in the war. Attlee's word power and rhetoric weren't as impressive. But the tone was the same. It was crisis time.

'I don't like it. Going to get a lot worse. Don't like it at all,' said my grandfather.

Was there no end to it? After the freezing February, March had been the wettest on record. A flood relief fund was started. Then there was yet more snow, more gales, more food shortages. Soon, we knew, the meat ration would be cut again.

'I'm going to emigrate if it goes on like this,' said Rowly, who blamed it all on the Labour government. 'What the country needs is a bloody lift.' No-one could find fault with that sentiment.

It came with the announcement that Princess Elizabeth was becoming engaged to Lt Philip Mountbatten, RN. They'd be getting married before the end of the year. The Princess was to be allowed one hundred clothing coupons for her wedding dress.

Mr Chapman arrived back from Rotary Club one Tuesday, very excited and more pink-cheeked than usual. He was twirling his rolled umbrella and noisily clearing his throat. That was the normal prelude to a pronouncement. The sub-editors' room looked up dutifully in anticipation.

His approach to journalism was above all staid and unsensational, devoid of that 'dreadful human interest' which he derided in the pages of the popular press. So what he had to say came as a surprise. He said he had discovered that very lunch hour that one of local Rotary's most revered members, a Yeovil shopkeeper of envied reputation, had a daughter who had just become engaged. Her name was also Elizabeth and her husband-to-be was in the Royal Navy.

'Oh dear me!' said Mr Chapman, quite overcome by the realisation that he had happened on a little scoop for the *Gazette*. 'It's difficult to know how we should tackle it. But I suppose we should, before these terrible evening papers get on to it. It is all rather delicate, however, because it touches royalty and one of the Rotary Club's most venerable members.'

It was beginning to sound to me slightly sick making, though not without its news value. He turned towards me. 'Do you think it's one I can risk you on, my boy? It would need to be written very tastefully. This young Elizabeth should be interviewed. I don't imagine you know her?'

I appeared to surprise him by saying that yes, I thought I did. In the interests of discretion, I chose not to question his description of her as young. She had never struck me that way. Despite persistence, guile and brazen enterprise, the impression she gave to most of my workmates was that she was slipping prematurely into nebulous middle-age, without a husband.

Not that it was for lack of sexual initiative on her part. Her doting father might have been blind to her insatiable proclivities – but certainly not the occupants of the reporters' room. One or two, I understood, knew her quite intimately. They were not in a minority.

'I believe she's a little older than the Princess but is still a good-looking woman. It's important to convey the sweet innocence of womanhood. . .' He broke off to bask in the sound of a phrase he would have seldom used. 'Yes, that is important. Remember, my boy, the royal romance has captured the imagination of the whole nation.'

'She. . . em. . . Yeovil's Elizabeth works in the family shop – up in the cash office, Mr Chapman. Shall I go and see her tomorrow?'

'I think so. Her father would like us to do something. And it's such a coincidence. I believe her husband-to-be is an officer in the Navy. Well, maybe a petty officer. You must check that. But ask the right questions. No silly evening-paper nonsense.'

'Just the facts, Mr Chapman,' I said, imprudently parodying my mentor.

'You are learning, young Matthew. Let me see now, check whether her mother is still an officer in the Soroptimists. Find out whether

97

Elizabeth is a member of St John's Church, like her father. . .'

It was yet another impossible briefing. But this was Mr Chapman's own special scoop, straight from the Rotary Club, and the story had to be done properly. Uncharacteristic words from him like Romance and Sweet Innocence of Womanhood played discordant, ironic notes in my ears.

I called at the shop next day. There were no customers and the assistant was painting her toenails, ready to peep with garish ugliness through her wedge shoes.

'Is Elizabeth in, please?'

'Up in the office. She's got someone up there with her but I didn't see who it was. Go on up. She's not too busy, I'm sure.'

Could it be that her big, brawny petty officer was on shore leave? That would be perfect. I could ask him all about himself at the same time.

I quietly walked up the wooden stairway. The cash office was to the right at the top. The door was closed.

I knocked and heard a voice which I assumed was saying 'Come in!' The door seemed to be sticking and I pushed it hard. It must have been locked – the bolt came off its hinges and the key clattered onto the floor.

There was Elizabeth stretched out in uncomfortable familiarity across the top of the wide desk, her skirt pushed high and her blouse undone. A man was clumsily climbing off her body. I'd have liked to think it was the petty officer. But it was Mr Franklin, the fishmonger from the next-door shop.

I apologised and retreated. Back at the office I told Mr Chapman it hadn't been convenient for Elizabeth to see me. Maybe it would be sensible after all for one of the senior reporters to take over the story.

Mr Chapman peered at me over his glasses. 'Yes, well yes, young Matthew. I think that would be wise. You're still young, inexperienced – just a wee bit too much so to understand what's involved in a happy, uplifting story like this. We must get it absolutely right – told in a way which will appeal to our readers and also catch the mood of true romance.

'I want Elizabeth's father to be able to come up to me at next week's Rotary and tell me how proud he is of his daughter. . .'

SEVEN

Vintage Summer

O N A SUMMER'S EVENING, when I wasn't working late in the office, I could cycle home, bolt down my plate of salad, change my trousers and, from a sense of unspoken duty, help my father in the garden for an hour or so. Only occasionally did I feel the need to invent an assignment. Gardening was never a bind for me. I loved the feel of the finely raked soil on my fingers as I hard-weeded, just as I relished the subtle smells of the herbs. As I forked out the couch or thinned the beetroot, my head was invariably going helter-skelter in pursuit of a dozen dreams. Like an old tabby rolling rapturously in the rough, warm earth, I found an instant serenity whenever I moved between the little avenues of stretching hollyhocks, the hoe slung in mannered preparedness across my still slim shoulders.

The perfumes of the garden were heady stimuli. Even the weeds had a scent all their own, just like those incandescent occupants of the flower borders that my parents tended with such fond and patterned care. This was 1947 and Eliot's East Coker was surging into rich bloom again. The wisteria tumbled playfully over the Ham-stone garden walls. Red Admiral butterflies fluttered from the buds, wheeling and soaring high as the thatched roofs. Exotic shrubs in the adjoining Paddock flirted with my twitching nostrils. The solitary poplar there, high as Tellis Hill, swayed her tantalising hips, demanding in that slender, beguiling arrogance that the visitor should pause and admire such delicate sensuality.

As long as I could remember, old men of the village, wizened, rheumaticky, had leaned over their small, wooden, white-painted front gates which led onto the stone steps across the narrow stream. I would stop to chat, or more often to listen. They had weatherbeaten faces, an innocence, dignity and air of simple contentment which masked the pain from their aching joints. They, to me, were the world's true philosophers. They would talk, unself-consciously, about the mysterious fluctuations of the season, the climate, country animals and the vagaries of nature. They dispensed rustic proverbs with catarrhal chuckles as they pulled on their clay pipes. Their bodies were twisted with old age and the cumulative grind of manual work. They had few real possessions except their vast reserve of wisdom. They were God-fearing, uncomplaining and, in some cases, illiterate in the accepted sense. Yet to me they were men of infinite education and knowledge. They couldn't define a logarithm and didn't know how to start making an atom bomb. But they knew, instead, why spring followed winter. They could grow onions as big as swedes; they sensed, without recourse to barometers, when the weather was going to change. Their obsessive affinity with nature didn't preclude a mischievous awareness in human foibles. 'Soon be a change at the vicarage, over at Chinnock, Matthew lad. Passon's all right. But 'ee do like that there wine too much, so they say. Pour out too much o' it and then there be plenty left over fer him. Our Gwen do say he's allus lickin' his chops at the end of the service.'

I was proudest of all when old Jack Neville would look at my hands after I'd been digging and hoeing for a couple of hours. 'You bin working, I can see. Half the 'lotment's under thee fingernails.' That was real acceptance.

In my village, a young man was judged, when it came to the elders at their front gates, by his fingernails. You didn't walk down the street to Mrs Ray's minute, paraffin-reeking little shop with clean hands. A Coker lad wore his pride on his fingers; it was a pride generated by centuries of ancestors who dirtied their hands as they sowed and reaped the vegetables for the bare kitchen table. Hands engrained with peasant soil were an emblem that I liked to keep on show. It represented my roots, my complexes. Some evenings, when I knew I had to see one of my elderly near-neighbours, I would secretly rub lumps of coal or craggy soil into my palms. My grandfather liked to see the grain of a hard day's manual work on my fingers. He said nothing but I would catch him looking at a countryman's nails with approval. Into his eighties, he bent with a grunt of pain to use his fingers instead of a hoe to remove an emerging dandelion. His nails were always long and black; he cut them once a week with his pocket knife.

It wouldn't have done for me to tell someone like Jack Neville that I worked for a newspaper and needed lily-white fingers and often a double-breasted suit. I liked him to think of me as a gardener. It had something to do with guilt, something I couldn't quite explain; it wasn't a pose. But each morning, before I went to work, I scrubbed vigorously to remove the coal dust and garden clay.

In that resurgent, voluptuous, blossoming summer, I was struck repeatedly by the thought that the old men at their gates were rare artists as well as philosophers. They had no need of easels; yet their exquisite brushwork was a wondrous harmony of vegetables and flowers, woven into a bewitching kaleidoscope that stretched out to every corner of the cottage garden. The seemingly higgledy-piggledy arrangement bloomed and flowered in a transformation of ordered colour that only an artist could have conceived. Marigolds and pansies twisted their way in a floral frieze alongside the narrow earth paths that meandered from back doors to the lavatories at the top of the garden. Sweet-williams were much favoured at East Coker. The stretching azurine delphiniums vied for attention with the more ostentatious peonies.

Never before or since was I so seduced by the sensuality of life. I had grown up sensitive enough to be touched by the natural beauty of my native village. The old stone cottages, draped in the velvety foliage of Virginia creeper, had quaint little windows, peeping out from under the thatch, often kept open in the summer time by a piece of string and a nail. The front stone steps were scrubbed daily till they shimmered in the morning sun. From the parish tower, the chimes sang out their tuneful greeting every three hours.

Only the newspapers and the wireless bulletins were the spoilsports. They were still going on about the uneasy peace. Bevin and Vishinsky were wagging their fingers at each other, there was the unhealthy heat of brimstone in the Security Council. But to me, East Coker was blissfully serene again. It had a kind of resilience to man's folly. The narrow country roads that snaked with indeterminate pattern around the thatched cottages were stained reassuringly by the dried dung spilled from countless carts through timeless generations.

My complexes of pubescence had disappeared. Emergent glimpses of a libidinous nature added to the excitement of growing up and becoming a man amid the unleashed joys of restored peace in this pastoral setting. The world stretched itself out in front of me, invitingly. I was in no mood to start questioning where things had gone wrong in 1939 or whether they were fundamentally any better now. The politicians were whispering that the ascetic Cripps, with that unyielding spiritual motivation of his, might soon be taking over as

Chancellor from Dalton – though that was in fact a transfer of power precipitated by a Budget indiscretion.

I didn't really want to know about that. Few boys of my age did. Our senses were in control. During those fleeting summer months of 1947, after the cold and the snow, life was for me as Utopian as it will ever be.

There was also Compton and Edrich. I listened to their monopolistic deeds on the cumbersome old wireless set perched on the kitchen table. How I loved that wireless set: how I panicked when the ironmonger was a day late with the recharged accumulator. For me it had been Stainless Stephen, Robb Wilton, Claude Dampier and Big-hearted Arthur. Now in 1947 it was *Much Binding* and *Variety Bandbox*. And Carroll Levis with his transatlantic voice and dreadful discoveries. And, of course, John Arlott, with the lovely novelty of his Basingstoke vowels as he caressed and garlanded every stroke of the Middlesex Twins with unpretentious poetry rather than the sterile verbiage straight from the BBC style-book.

Compton was my metaphor for the summer. The not noticeably Brylcreemed hair, tousled in the gentle breezes, symbolised what we hoped was an emerging new freedom. He loved the sun, as that tanned, smiling face showed. He was an adventurer, supremely confident: he went with almost skittish abandonment three yards down the wicket and still middled the ball. It was as if, to see him bounding towards 4,000 runs, he had rediscovered the Golden Age for us all to enjoy again.

He was handsome, daring, heroic. Yet he was marvellously ordinary, in his family and elementary school life. Village boys could privately identify with him while knowing in their hearts that he had to remain an intangible idol. The lightweight Compton bat described mesmeric arcs as it slanted and swirled. It never seemed to miss the ball. The coordination carried magnetism and magic. At times this most human of individuals appeared possessed of infallibility. Once as he went to play his shot, his boots spiked together and he was momentarily immobile. He flicked a flailing bat in the vague direction of the approaching ball and it scorched away for four. At the other end was his friend, Bill, the war hero. The chemistry between them that wondrous season was unique in the history of first-class cricket. Those who called them the Terrible Twins were the succession of bowlers made to look impotent. The same bowlers also grinned with good grace through their pain. I found Compton and Edrich uplifting rather than terrible.

I used to listen to Mr Arlott's latest account of their prodigious blows and then walk alone in the evening up past the
Tudor almshouses and the Norman church to the lofty, sprawling
parkland. The Park was my chosen retreat. From early boyhood, I'd
wandered there to gather chestnuts for the hob or triumphantly to
snap off the mushrooms as they peeped up through the glistening
early-morning dew.

There was a beloved sycamore, its thick lower branches bent
with age, which I could climb quite easily. I would expertly pick my
way twenty-five feet up and then sit astride my favourite bough, legs
dangling freely, to gaze down across the village. The sheer silence,
almost mystical, would enrapture me. There were still relatively few
cars on the road but every few minutes a farm cart or a tradesman's
van would rattle round the bends on its way to Yeovil. The noise was
an intrusion as it reverberated and throbbed a mile or so up the rough
hillside where I sat out of sight aloft my sycamore. That stillness of
evening on a hazy summer's day has remained for me an unrivalled
peak of sublime happiness, though never again quite capturing the
idyllic months of 1947.

I would eventually climb down from the old tree, gently caressing
the buttercups and celandines with my sandals or playfully tossing
a piece of dry wood as far as I could. Ground movements would
startle me but I'd realise they were no more than the muffled sound
of snoozing Shorthorns shifting their languid limbs. My gaze would
return to the parish below me. If the summer nights were beginning
to get chilly, I would see the smoke from a dozen cottage chimneys
slanting at the same precise angle to indicate the direction of the
faint eventide wind.

This vast parkland, sprawling out from the boundary hedges of the
manor house, was my haven. I shared it with the slumbering cows.
It was also my county headquarters – not Lord's or The Oval because
those institutions of first-class cricket rarely touched me emotionally,
but Taunton. Taunton was intimate and snug, with the distinctive
white fencing close enough for us to joke with the square-leg umpire.
It was full of country voices and rosy-cheeked boys with school satchels
bulging with spam sandwiches rather than Latin declensions. There
were Walls ice creams and the romantic, imagined smell of heather
drifting down from the Quantock backdrop. My park was Taunton
in high summer. Compton and Edrich were usually batting – and I
was bowling, cunning off-breaks, pitching just outside off stump and
ever threatening to nibble at the leg-side bail. Esteemed reputations

were at stake; it was no time to be squeamish. I would pick up a dried cow-pat, roll it approximately into a ball and bowl on a length towards the sturdy trunk of the sycamore. Compton was inclined to match guile with guile. He would prance down the wicket to stifle the spin and shoot me a half-wicked, half-appreciative grin. Edrich would pull with a taunting cross-bat until I endangered his cavalier approach with revised deployment of my fielders and use of a stealthy short mid-wicket. It was always a mutually intelligent contest.

My own, more realistic, cricket – transported from the Elysian flights of dreamland – was limited. Most Saturdays I was expected to set off on my three-speed around the fête and flower-show circuit. There were at least three of these monumentally dreary events to cover each weekend. It was in no sense a journalistic experience; our ordered duty was simply to take down an interminable list of prize-winners and organising committee. People bought the *Gazette* to see their name there. If the marquee burnt down, I felt with increasing cynicism, the calamity might have earned a grudging mention at the foot of the report. The fact that Lady Blenkinsop had opened the fête and that Mrs Huggins had won 'the economical cake class' (signs of the times) were expected to be given precedence.

On one of those rare Saturdays when I wasn't working, I'd volunteer to play cricket for either the *Western Gazette* or East Coker. The *Gazette* had the better fixtures but our home matches were played halfway to Sherborne and that meant for most of us a testing, debilitating cycle ride up the Alpine-like Babylon Hill to get there. We needed to flop out on the grass in exhaustion when we reached the ground. It was no suitable physical preparation for a challenging duel with the sturdy seafaring men of Lyme Regis or those seemingly well-heeled lawyers and surveyors from Castle Cary. The visitors usually won – before the match started.

I was happier playing for East Coker. The team was composed of gregarious village lads back from the war, and old friends from the local council school. There was more of a cultural affinity. We could shed social graces and exchange hoary jokes about our forefathers and past denizens of parish life. We'd guffaw with affection when someone mentioned Tom Hackwell, the local undertaker whose prospects of improved trade were evident when Tammy Neville was letting a few wild ones go, fast-medium, on practice night. And then there was Herbie Dodge. He'd had a trial for Somerset and should have played. He was a fine upright batsman with a penchant for the unorthodox. His most productive shot was a four to long leg, achieved by leaning back, lifting his left leg and somehow in defiance of logic, sweeping the ball under a lofted limb.

With the arrogance of youth I looked on myself as an all-rounder. 'If you can get off work to play against Evershot on Saturday, you can open the batting and the bowling,' said Eddie, my captain, in tones more of desperation than flattery. He was struggling to round up eleven able-bodied sportsmen.

It coincided with the annual Women's Institute flower show at East Coker. My enthusiasm for matters journalistic was temporarily on the wane, as I recall. I had turned in a graphic account of the killing of an adder but it warranted no more than three lines with the sensational 12-point headline: HARMLESS SNAKE KILLED. Why did some know-all have to write in and say it was only a grass snake? I'd guessed it might be. But I was seventeen by now and was proficient enough at my craft to know that adders wriggling through the snapdragons in residential Yeovil were likely to make better copy.

I had also had the good professional fortune to be walking on the pavement outside Beswick's the fish-and-chip shop two hundred yards from the *Gazette* building when a pan of fat caught fire and there was much panic among the staff, preparing for opening time.

I weighed up the possibilities of the adjoining shops and houses going up in flames, stifled my disappointment when the Brigade arrived to discover the fire was already out and wandered back to the office.

'Could have been nasty, Mr Chapman. Some of the neighbours were thinking of evacuating. Yes, very nasty for a few minutes.'

My mentor, a former district reporter, had probably written hundreds of one-paragraph stories about minor fires. 'Just a chip pan, young Matthew. It happens all the time. Gerald can pick the details up from the Brigade in the morning.'

If the *Gazette* didn't want an eye-witness account of blazing haddock, then they might have to take second best when it came to the East Coker flower show. I spoke confidentially to Winnie, the jolly WI secretary, embroidered the complications of a busy Saturday and asked if I might pick up from her the long list of prize-winners on the Sunday morning. Winnie wasn't privy to the current selection of the local cricket club. Her husband was hot favourite to win the challenge cup for most points in the show. I made a mental memo that his horticultural exploits would be generously recorded.

Evershot was a new fixture. Transport was always a problem for impecunious village clubs like ours in the immediate postwar years, and this particular sortie into Hardy's Dorset countryside was too far for bicycles. But one of the team suddenly showed untold enterprise. He worked at the village sawmill and, I hope – but rather doubt – with the acquiescence of his employers, he thought he might be able to borrow one of the lorries. It was a vehicle more often used for the rough and ready movement of two-ton tree trunks.

Our driver turned up with an excessively dramatic screeching of brakes at our normal meeting place, alongside 'The Tree' at 1.30pm. Two of the more senior members of the team squeezed in alongside him. The rest of us clambered with difficulty up onto the open back. There were no sides and I feared for safety standards.

We had thrown up our confined assortment of discoloured bats and bedraggled pads, mostly bereft of straps. There was nothing as sophisticated as a cricket bag. If we had a bat of our own, we brought it – to be shared. No-one, as far as I knew, possessed a box or the merest evidence of protective gear. Our more immediate preoccupation was in keeping the swirling sawdust out of our eyes on that awful, lurching ride to Evershot. We bounced haplessly like beach balls, battering and bruising our buttocks, as the sawmill lorry's pragmatic tyres hit every undulation on the country lanes. We hung on, with pallid complexions and fixed expressions of phoney good humour, to each other.

'Fer Chrissake, Len – take yer bloody foot off the 'celerator. Me ass is bruised to buggery. And we han't even met they Evershot fellers yet,' someone yelled to an unhearing driver.

By the time we got to the ground, we were in an advanced, collective state of bleeding haemorrhoids. We were also convinced our sight had been permanently impaired by the frenzied, unabated storm of sawdust.

The wicket itself had been cut, more or less; the outfield, as far as we could see, not at all. 'Don't chuck thee bat down in the grass, the'll lose it in t'undergrowth'. It seemed to be a valid warning, we didn't have any bats to spare. But the home team, burly and rubicund, were hospitable enough. We lost the toss and picked our way, through the giant dandelions with stalks like pea-stickers, to the wicket.

Village cricketers are adept at earthy psychology. The Evershot team allowed us to eavesdrop on the exuberantly imparted news that they were without exception in good nick. There were several farmers in the side and there was a recurrent theme in jocular and boastful vein that they would be knocking up a quick fifty before nipping home to do the afternoon milking.

Bill, our regular wicket-keeper, hadn't apparently passed himself as fit enough for his normal ponderously brilliant leg-side stumpings, and came along as umpire instead. A non-playing umpire was a rare luxury for us. We made much of it as Bill put on the white coat. He was also a loyal pal of mine and my family. During the blackout, in the early years of the war before he went into the Navy, he used to cycle two miles from his home, a heavy bagatelle table resting on his head and steadied by one hand, for us all to share an evening's innocent fun.

We went out to field and the skipper honoured his promise. He threw me the ball. Coker CC never bothered its head too much about the niceties of a conventional seam attack. I affected to spin the ball from the off, whether on the approximation of a square, discoloured and lushly manured by the plentiful excretions of Farmer Denning's sheep, at East Coker, or a grassy stretch of meadowland in Dorset. But I was permitted no illusions about the importance of my role as a bowler. 'You'm goin' on fust becus thee'st keep a length.' Spin didn't come into it.

I always felt such lack of appreciation of my subtleties was a pity. That afternoon I took seven wickets for six runs. It was real Tom Goddard stuff and the feat would possibly still be in the village's cricketing records – if it had been in the nature of the lads in our club to tabulate and cherish our weekly deeds. The good performances were extolled and relived when we had a pint mug in our hands. Then they receded, to be partially lost or affectionately embroidered in the haze of distant memory.

The undulating, rustic wicket was conducive to my twitching fingers. I held the seam one way and then the other. No-one had ever taught me to cut the ball away but that was what I found I was occasionally doing as a variation to my turn-the-door-handle spinners. Three of my victims were leg-before, though I can't accept the implication of several Evershot batsmen that I leaned on the friendship of a compliant umpire. Now I come to the reason why I remember the match so vividly. It has nothing at all to do with my Goddard imitation.

A mounting atmosphere of inter-parish antipathy was reached when I had one of their early batsmen out lbw second ball. He was a big, red-faced, broad-shouldered man, who wore bulging prewar flannels, hitched up at the waist by a thick farm-labourer's belt. His bat was virginal white, acquired only the week before. My pace and approach were enticingly ingenuous and the second ball must have been destined, as he saw it, for the front lawn of Lord Ilchester's estate nearby. But somehow the ball eluded the crudely flailing bat and thudded against those massive off-white pads which obscured all three stumps. My appeal was that of a confident young man who had long forgotten his days as a boy soprano at St Michael's. 'Bagatelle' Bill, much impressed and no doubt surprised by my ability to beat that heaving bat, put up his finger even before I was halfway through my highly vocal entreaty. Neither of us could have foreseen the consequences.

The batsman stood transfixed. His mouth was open, unspeaking, in disbelief. Then, within five seconds, it turned to anger. Bill wasn't having any nonsense. He summoned up a sense of authority for the looming crisis. He put up his finger a second time and said: 'You're out, old son.' The garage owner put his hands on his hips and stayed his ground. 'Don't be so damn silly. Course I weren't out.'

'You was.' The response had an air of finality.

But the batsman's protestations became oaths. He advanced a few steps down the wicket. He raised his bat in what I took to be a threatening position. I was convinced he was going to strike either Bill or myself. He had gone puce in the face. Then he came forward again, unsteady in his rage, and stopped just short of us. He was the tallest man on his side and now he towered in menace above the intrepid bowler and umpire. I could feel the heat from his nostrils, or maybe I just imagined that.

'Wos mean, I was out?'

'Cus you was.'

'Wos wrong with yer eyes. It weren't goin' to hit they stumps. And I baint goin'. Bloody umpires!'

Bill didn't flinch. It was a display of phlegm *par excellence*. 'Get on back. You're out.' He lit a Woodbine, there at his station, and just waited for the next man to come in. The exchange turned into a monologue. It went on for three or four minutes and it seemed to me, as I pondered the impasse of which I'd been the instigator, that the match might have to be abandoned.

Most of us sat on the grass as the two batsmen went into a huddle, punctuated by more oaths and slanderous imputations directed at poor old Bill. My friend continued inhaling deeply on his Woodbine and surveying Hardy's sylvan countryside on all sides of him with extravagant unconcern. Eventually, the aggrieved batsman, placated by his more temperate partner, trudged by a devious, distracted route back to the little pavilion. It was the nearest to physical violence I ever saw on a cricket ground. I found it decidedly uncomfortable, only comical in retrospect. I think I'd have preferred to face Hall and Griffith a few years later.

After that, Charlie – a cynical old war veteran with a beer-gut, broken marriage and warm heart – and I quickly ran through the rest of the Evershot innings. Charlie was also slowish and accurate. We felt like Coker's Horace Hazell and Johnny Lawrence. . . with smarting bloodshot eyes. The wonder was that we were even able to make out the distant stumps after all that swirling sawdust. 'Could have done with a bloody guide dog,' said Charlie.

'And a bit of armour plating,' I added with a coward's shiver.

The match was over by teatime. The teams didn't exactly fraternize. We paid our one-and-sixpence for the lettuce sandwiches and shallots. But countrymen from rival parishes and counties don't harbour a grudge for long, certainly not when opening time is approaching. Conversation was tentatively renewed and then by common will cordiality restored. We all had a drink together, well nearly all of us. I wanted – naive youth though I may have been – to buy my inconsolably 'wronged' batsman a pint. But he'd already gone.

Long before the sawmill lorry had rattled home, most of us had forgotten the brimstone in the long grass. All was 1947 peace and serenity again. Charlie, taciturn by nature, was now loudly proclaiming that he really was as fast as Voce and could make the ball wobble around in the air like a kite lurching languidly in the gentle breeze of a hazy, Dorset afternoon. Bill was saying he'd be leaving the umpiring to Frank Chester in future and would be getting back to wicket-keeping where you could rely on a better relationship with the batsman.

I lay in bed on the Sunday morning, thinking that there would never be another war and that Denis Compton would make runs for ever. I'd heard Herbert Morrison, on the wireless, going on about tightening our belts still more, and Clem Attlee talking in that dreary way of his about the Government's Austerity Plan. It should have troubled me but it didn't. I knew Attlee was a good bloke and I could trust him – because he liked cricket and was apt to tell us we should play down the line with a straight bat in moments of national crisis.

'They'm goin' to ration tiddies next. Shouldn't wonder if 'tis bacon next. They'm talking of halvin' the rashers,' said my grandfather, when I went across the road for a brief Sunday-morning chat and a furtive look at his *News of the World*. I could never tell why he took it. *News Chronicle* and worthy items of international news all week, the big black Bible there for ever, on the corner of the old table, next to the Quaker Oats: and then the plethora of saucy court stories on Sunday. He used to read it slowly, intently without visible reaction, during the afternoon. After that the Bible was opened. He would readily express an opinion on the state of the nation, the needs of more wartime rationing and the virtues of nationalisation, never a text from the Good Book. If there was moralising to be done, he considered it was up to my parents.

I checked the back page to ascertain the inevitable, another hundred from Compo. There was also an action picture of Edrich. It made me think of one of him I'd seen in *Picture Post* during the war. He was a Squadron Leader and was running for his plane. The caption wasn't allowed to identify him; it described him as 'a well-known Test cricketer'. From Compton and Edrich, I moved on to the erring curates on the centre pages. Then it was time to collect my three-speed from under the yew tree at the top of the garden, and cycle off to see Winnie, the local Women's Institute secretary.

I hummed a Dinah Shore number. The prospect of seeing the luscious Jean Kent in *Good Time Girl* at the Odeon on the Monday evening was very much in my mind – but, in truth, not as much as the lingering romance of my 7 for 6 in the pretty little field of long grass at Evershot. It was a good, sunny Sunday morning, full of country smells and marigold front-gardens. How could one expect a teenage boy to be obsessed with the daunting economics of the nation? Instead, I thought again of Jean Kent. There had been talk of bringing her down to Yeovil as the special guest for the Press Ball. I already had plans to take Diana. Jean Kent and Diana in one evening: my head and loins registered in unison.

Winnie made me a cup of tea, as I copied out the complete lists of winners from the previous day's flower show. Arthur, her husband, had won the cup again. I was profuse with my congratulations, extending with psychological cunning the biographical notes in conscientious Pitman's over a page and a half. To my surprise, my father came first with his vegetable marrows and onions. They were always whoppers. I privately put it down to the fact that you couldn't beat human excrement when it came to organic manure. Dad would empty the two-holed lavatory, at the top of the garden, twice a year. It was a reluctant, but necessary labour. He would undo a hatch let into the brickwork, and shovel the collective waste matter of the family into a wheelbarrow. It was then hurriedly and discreetly buried in various parts of the vegetable patch.

Dad was always proud of the quality of his crops. 'Lot of goodness in the ground,' he'd say. 'Can't beat Jack Mead's farmyard manure.' And his friends who knew him well would dig him in the ribs and add: 'Topped up wi' a few loads of they Fouracres' recycled shit!'

My report, thanks to Winnie, was comprehensive. It listed the gate-stewards, the stallholders, the organising committee and the dozens of prize-winners, first, second and third. Mechanically I recorded that the show was held as usual in the grounds of North Coker House, by kind permission of Mrs C.C. Maudslay. According to the helpful Winnie, Mrs Maudslay, who had also declared the show open, had spoken of the importance of growing our own vegetables in a time of national food shortage. That at least gave me a topical paragraph to precede that mountain of names.

As an emergent democrat, I considered it was just as crucial to the proceedings to mention that 'the day was rounded off with dancing in the Village Hall, to Stan Russell and his Trio.' I liked Stan, a village boy with thick, stubby fingers but an undeniable sense of syncopation that I was apt to bracket with Charlie Kunz. Stan kept it in the family; his wife played the drums. He had taught her to use the brushes ('Just keep time, no clever stuff, love'). Stan had his trusted repertoire and didn't often wander from it. He played by ear. I'm not sure if he read music but in any case you didn't go in for complicated Glenn Miller orchestrations when all you had was a piano, sax and drum. Stan thumped more as the night went on, with numbers of dancers increasing after the New Inn had come out. He and the sax player bashed out the familiar melody; Glad cut out the clever stuff and looked after the tempo. 'Whispering' and 'Marjie' were their best quicksteps. It occasionally went to Stan's head as he soared into the treble clef, keeping time as he hammered the pedal with his polished right shoe, and imagining he was Art Tatum.

On the Monday, after I'd handed in my report, I was told: 'We could have done with a bit more from Mrs Maudslay about the food shortage. Did she say anything else? Got your notebook with you, have you?'

Rowly, who when he didn't have a thick head could eavesdrop on three conversations at the same time as he sub-edited a village cup match, asked: 'Did she have a go at that sodding Labour government?'

No, I quickly said, I didn't have my notebook with me – and no, she didn't go into politics. 'Well, she bloody well should have,'

Rowly went on. 'She's chairman of the local Women's Conservative Association.'

'Only said a few words, I'm afraid. I took down every one,' I fibbed.

On the following day I had a great stroke of luck. I was opening the editorial post. One of the envelopes, addressed to the sports editor, contained a brief report from a village correspondent in Dorset of a cricket match between Evershot and East Coker on the Saturday. It contained the damning evidence that 'a young journalist, M. Fouracre, playing for East Coker, was in fine form to take 7 for 6 with his off-spinners and was twice on a hat trick.'

My reaction was an amalgam of pride and panic. I dithered and then panic realistically won. With great reluctance I obliterated my achievement with a thick lead pencil, before passing over the report.

EIGHT

The Last Waltz

URING MY eighteen months or so as a copy boy, made
endurable only by my rare sorties into the reporters' room,
I had become adept at a succession of minor art forms –
addressing district men's envelopes at frenetic two-fingered speed,
detecting with an uncanny facility the varying footsteps of the girls
from the reading room as they descended the stairs, and acquiring a
working knowledge of Gerald's medication for a spectrum of anxieties
that now encompassed asthma and hay fever as well as feared disor-
ders of the genitalia. Such skills were, of course, over and above my
necessary proficiency as proof-puller, tea-maker, files-updater,
tobacco-buyer, news parcels-collector (at the town station on Mon-
days and Thursdays at 6.30am) and human buffer during the frequent
exchanges between the editorial and advertisement departments.

My professional progress was assessed mainly, it appeared to me,
by the crisp cleanness of the proofs I presented on request from my
superiors and by the absence of typing errors on the letters that my
news editor dictated to me. Presumptuously I would at times improve
the grammar and simplify the surfeit of subordinate clauses.

It would be quite wrong of me to say that my year and a half, on
that little side table, downwind of Clev's raging baccy smoke, where
between summonses I studied my shorthand and read steamy snatches
of D.H. Lawrence, was wholly wasted. The old-style indoctrination
and insistence on 'accuracy above all' could be irksome. In the same
way, I rather resented being told incessantly: 'You're coming on quite
well, my lad. One day you will be sent out to cover County Court
and maybe the Town Council. Just think of that!'

I thought of it, often, as I retreated for lavatorial elevenses – and
it horrified me. That kind of working pattern just didn't square with
my private aspirations of making my way to Fleet Street, and then

113

going round with an 'Arfer' Helliwell titfer on the back of my head and a beer-stained gaberdine mac, belted tightly at the waist.

I had to accept that the *Gazette* was a good paper. No weekly in the country had a bigger circulation – 'over five counties, don't you forget it, Matthew. . . and into every home.' It had an infallible ear for what its readers wanted. They didn't want flash journalism and racy human-interest angles. I didn't think that in the long term it was for me.

Maybe my head was too full of newspaper fiction and preconceived notions. My idols were the men and women who wrote one-sentence paragraphs and had their famous bylines at the top of the story. When I was still at school, a kindly old clergyman who had heard I was hankering for a job in journalism, surprised me by saying I should read the Bible more often. 'Plenty of drama and human interest there. And very well written, my boy. Short sentences. You can't beat them.'

The *Gazette* went in for interminable sentences. There was one sub, the son of the editor, who with almost paranoiac relish would transform up to seven or eight sentences into one. He was even known to take two paragraphs, already of inordinate length, and somehow bridge them with yet another conjunction. It was apparently a matter of literary pride for him. He had an expensive, thick-nibbed fountain pen and would scatter his infernal armoury of short, repetitive conjunctions all over the folios of typed copy. At the end of his joinery, he'd survey his handiwork and re-read his convoluted coil of words with visible satisfaction. The editorials sometimes ran for nine hundred words and I swear there was seldom a new paragraph.

The tutelage extended to me was well-meaning but apt to be worthless. 'We must get you writing a little better, mustn't we? Must improve the style. See how we do it in the *Gazette* every week – that's the proper way to write. We can't have you doing those silly short sentences. Oh dear, no. You must think you're Edgar Wallace or something!'

I suspect that Cherry, in more youthful and less inhibited days, must have furtively read Wallace. It was a frequent joke of his, when one of the more stereotyped district reporters got above himself with a flight of fanciful prose. 'Now then, we can't have too many Edgar Wallaces on the staff, can we?'

My only wry conclusion was that the thriller writer earned rather more than my twenty-five bob a week, as he pulled on his long cigarette holder and dictated his laconic narrative to a secretary. But my mounting frustration, creative rather than financial, was about to be eased.

'Let's see, how long have you been with us, Matthew?'

'Eighteen months or more, Mr Chapman.'

'Ah yes, well perhaps it's time to see what you can really do. You will know that we have recently lost one of our senior reporters at head office.' Here, my mentor shook his head, pausing to administer one last silent rebuke to the departing newsman. 'He will regret it, of course. He had some wonderful prospects here. I honestly don't know, young Matthew, what he was thinking about.' Once more he broke off, to look me disconcertingly in the eyes. 'I am appointing another copy boy. He will be starting on Monday. And you will move into the reporters' room.'

My enthusiasm, or maybe I should say relief, was boundless. 'That's terrific, Cher – em – Mr Chapman. I've been hoping – '

'Your pay will be going up to thirty shillings a week. And don't forget that we have our non-contributory provident fund. We look after our staff. We like them to stay with us for a lifetime.'

Stuart's move, the move indeed of any member of the editorial staff, was seen by the unwaveringly loyal assistant editor as nothing short of betrayal. 'We kept his place open for when he came back from the war, you know. He could have ended up. . . in my shoes. Or even higher.'

I looked down. Those shoes glistened, still fresh from the morning's Cherry Blossom. They were shoes fit to grace any sanctum of Rotarians. They were well-soled, solid, reliable, unadventurous. Stuart's were brown and more daring. He'd gone off to join the BBC in Bristol. He would never be quite forgiven.

The new copy boy had also come from my grammar school. His name was Durban. He had a sturdy build, a slight stammer and a hitherto unheard-of regard, at that lowly level of provincial journalism, for classical music. He would come into the office humming Sibelius. *Finlandia* was heavy stuff for the first few hours, while Rowly was still expelling through the varying apertures the remnants of Bruttons wind from the previous night. Gerald and myself, of a more philistine nature, were soon to discover to our relief that Durban was capable of manifesting an equal affection for carnal delights.

He did make the mistake, however, of revealing fairly quickly to his professional elders the interest he had in good music. On only the second Saturday of his employment, when plans had already been made for a modest bacchic excursion around a few of the less salubrious haunts of Reckleford and Park Street, he found himself pencilled in the diary for his first assignment. It was a recital of organ music at Holy Trinity Church, to be given by the husband of the regular organist. His name was not unknown to us; he was our diffident advertising manager, who chose to keep his fingers soft and supple by milking his goats through the week. To our knowledge he had only taken up the organ two years before. This was to be, in effect, his public debut though he had once nervously deputised for his sick wife on Rogation Sunday. The recital was given a polite twenty lines in the following Friday's paper and Durban was offered muted congratulations. He confided to the rest of the reporters that he had crept out just before the interval. He was learning fast.

The winter months were coming up again. I didn't really enjoy them. When it rained I wore a thick yellow oilskin as I cycled the four miles in from East Coker, often in the pitch dark with only a flickering torchlight to guide me away from the high hazel hedges on both sides. In bad weather the journey seemed twice as long. On the way home, there was a long, laborious haul up Hendford Hill. Those nights when I felt particularly weary, I would cycle just one hundred yards up the hill and wait for the next National bus to come along. It always slowed and changed gear at about this point where I was leaning on my machine. Then as soon as I was out of sight of the driver, I would throw my leg over the crossbar and grasp the luggage ladder at the back of the bus. I would then be pulled the whole way, nearly a mile, to the summit. In those days there was often a police constable at the top, outside the Quicksilver Mail. Experience taught me to let go of the luggage ladder just short of his vantage point.

In the postwar Forties, villages offered little in the way of social life, apart from whist drives and perhaps oldtime dancing, on weekdays during the winter. I spurned such hedonistic distractions. My inclination was to stay as long as possible in Yeovil after work. I saw The Corn is Green three times and Maugham's The Razor's Edge twice. I went into the few local cafés as a matter of rotation rather than choice. They offered nothing more enticing than spam sandwiches and rock cakes. Their tea was weak and the stained tablecloths were given an even rougher surface from the cumulatively spilled sugar. The windows were always steamed up and we used to draw faces and write rude words with our fingers on the panes.

The Press Ball was coming up and I felt I should go for the first time, if I could improve on the clumsy, basic steps induced by Stan Russell's up-tempo rendition of 'Marjie'. This caused me to consider investing a few florins in Sidney Samson's dancing classes which he held twice a week in a rented wooden hut.

'Who are you going to take to the Press Ball, sweetheart. I'd love to think it was me – but I daresay you've got someone else in mind,' Diana teased.

I had absolutely no-one else in mind. Sadly I knew by this time that she had. Gradually she had confided to me that she was living with an Italian ex-prisoner-of-war. He was doing all sorts of work, including an early-morning milk round, and saving hard so that he could return to a good job in Italy or with his relatives in America. Eventually he wanted to take Diana with him. One day, as I drank coffee with my mates at the Cadena, she called me across to the window. A milk van was parked in the side street. I saw her Italian return with an empty crate. He was handsome and very big. I could tell she was very much in awe of him, certainly frightened of him. I was afraid, too.

We used to go on meeting with almost comic discretion every ten days or so. She remained tender, the teacher. She teased mercilessly, giggling as I did my gauche best to pretend I wasn't embarrassed. She was a congenital flirt. Her lips were consciously moist and often half open, even when I was talking. Her repartee was sharp and cheeky, laced with sexual nuance, but the eloquence came from her body. In the cinema, she continued to find with wonderful intuition the deserted row. She would slide deep into her seat and then lift both legs high up across my thighs.

She used to tell me I was good for her. It was a flattering thing to hear – and yet almost as if she needed me, innocent and uncomplicated as I was, to mitigate the Latin excesses of her handsome milkman. Her curiosity about my work was utterly genuine. She liked all the reporters who came in for coffee; she found us more fun, and perhaps more randy, than the cross section of male clientele that sampled the mid-morning coffee beans.

'Maybe I'm not quite grand enough for the Press Ball. Evening dress and all that. Perhaps you feel I'm not quite right for that.'

It wasn't in any sense blackmail or play-acting. I hugged her as I shared her with Stewart Granger in *The Lamp Still Burns*.

'How can you get away from your Italian?'

'I'll think of something. . . The date's already in my diary, sweetheart.' I normally hated those corny terms of endearment. From Diana they seemed natural and intimate.

I polished up my quickstep and slow foxtrot at Sidney Samson's academy of dancing. His wife, a younger woman, took all the beginners in turn. That alone was worth the florin. She always wore a floral summer dress, sleeveless and with a generous V-neck, even in the middle of winter. She encouraged us to press our bodies against hers. 'I have to lean back at this angle and you must come over me like this.' She'd rather too eagerly ease us into position. Such advice was whispered in our ear – to all of us as we queued up for the privilege.

She must have boosted business enormously among the young male population of the town. Her legs were bare and shapely, accentuated – like Diana's on the first evening I took her out – by high heels. The legs were also strong and she brushed them against ours rather more than was necessary by the strictest interpretation of the Sylvester manual.

'Have you thought about going in for any of the exams?'

'Never going to be that good. And in any case, it's my work.'

'Try not to give up, dear. You move so nicely. And you've got a lovely, strong grip,' she cooed.

Sidney meanwhile did most of the instructing and put on the strict-tempo records. I would see him glancing as his wife went into fervent demonstration with another novice. It was hard to tell whether his eyes betrayed jealousy or commercial admiration.

The academy in the small wooden hut prepared me and built my confidence for the Press Ball. It was quite a social occasion for Yeovil, held in the Manor Hotel and attended by the mayor and mayoress. The committee had paid George Crow, well known for his radio broadcasts, £100 to bring a ten-piece orchestra. Hy Hazell, not Jean Kent after all, was the special guest. Her entourage from the film studios hardly left her side. It was all spectacular stuff, superseding for me, as in a fantasy, the dowdiness of the town's immediate postwar years.

At half past eight, as arranged, Diana arrived at the gravel drive of the hotel. She stepped out of a shabby, functional taxi, gazing for a moment uncertainly about her and protecting her hair from the November wind with a hand. I hadn't known what to expect. She was wearing a black half-length evening dress, both meretricious and attractive. The haughtier echelons on Yeovil's social scene would perhaps have sniffed at what they saw as its lack of elegance and taste. To me it was quite bewitching.

Her lips were bright, shiny red, grinning in a nervous way. The cleavage was discreetly daring. The perfume was strong. I stood there awkwardly, in my borrowed, frayed dress suit with cheap clip-on bow tie slanting at rather more than forty-five degrees. I was in no state to evaluate, in a dispassionate way, whether her presence belonged to an exclusive dance floor or a bordello. I was transfixed. She took my arm and we walked in together. I could feel her trembling.

I'd never been to a ball before. It seemed a very grand affair, with bony, self-conscious girls swirling round in their stiff long dresses, revelling in the self-delusion that they were used to this kind of glamour. George Crow's brass section sounded just like Ambrose or Geraldo on the wireless. I didn't care that he may have found half of them earlier in the day touting for work in Archer Street. They were real musicians. I watched how between the numbers the leader sifted through a pile of orchestrations, resting on the piano, and then passed round the band parts. Then they would actually read the music intently as they played. I never saw the Stan Russell Trio doing that.

I didn't know what to get Diana to drink, and she wasn't sure. So I brought her a big sweet sherry. I was now a man and thought a pint of bitter was right for me. We returned with our drinks to the edge of the dance floor. While she gazed at the dancers, I gazed at her. She was glowing with visible pleasure – and I basked in her enjoyment. When she caught me looking at her we both grinned without saying anything. The comic discomforture caused by my misshapen dress suit was soon forgotten. I sensed that for the first time in my life I was in love.

My older journalistic colleagues gave me glances of envy; if a few of them were contrived, I didn't care. Their ribald comments, as they bumped against us on the dance floor, brought more giggles from Diana. In the Gents, between dances, Rowly, flushed and belching happily in the next cubicle, said: 'Done all right for yourself, son. Where d'you pick her up? Been trying to look down her front all night.'

Diana and I danced the last waltz, very close, hardly moving. Emboldened by the dipped lights, my pints of bitter and the sensuous artificiality of the early hours at the Manor, I pulled her even tighter to me. 'You're getting the idea,' she whispered.

I took her home in a taxi. 'That was a lovely night. One of the best I've ever had,' she said, as we nestled in the hard back seat.

'But – but what about your Italian?'

'He's been away to see some friends in London. I'm not expecting him back till Sunday. . . . I want you to come home with me tonight.'

There was a long silence, full of words. We just looked at each other. I could still hear George Crow playing that dreamy last waltz, could still feel Diana's body, warm, barely moving, as a romantic old lyricist asked: *Who's taking you home tonight?* Hearing those words of invitation from Diana in the taxi, I was in some confusion. I wasn't absolutely sure what was happening to me. But I still had a damn good idea.

'Stop at the end of the next road,' she said to the driver. 'You won't need to wait for my friend. He's. . . coming in for a cup of tea.'

The taxi fare was fifteen shillings and I gave the driver a pound. In my present state, I'd have given him a fiver. We walked, holding hands, in the blurred moonlight – along the row of silent council houses. Suddenly Diana froze. She gripped my hand tightly and in almost the same movement released it. A man was leaning against the gate of the next house. I just knew it was her Italian milkman. He was tall, gaunt and forbidding.

'I didn't think. . . didn't think you'd be back until – '

He said nothing. He opened the gate, took her arm and led her in. She half looked back, wanting to say something. No words came out.

I was left on the pavement, alone. The light went on in a back room but I could hear no sound. There was nothing for me to do. Full of unease, fearful, desperately unfulfilled, I began the walk back towards the centre of the town, grateful that an empty taxi saw me and pulled up.

Next morning in the office, there was the usual post mortem on the Ball. Whatja think of the band? Whatja think of Hy Hazell? And from Gerald: Did you get your end away?

Just after eleven, I received a phone call. It was from Diana. She sounded strained. Could I see her in half an hour at the Victoria Café? She very much hoped I could. I was there in twenty minutes, apprehensively waiting for her when she came in. She was pale, without make-up or her normal flirtatious spark. Her eyes were red as if she'd been crying all night. I could see what looked like a bruise high on one cheek.

'I've come to say goodbye, sweetheart.'

B-picture dialogue again, maybe – but I also knew it was real enough. I couldn't quite articulate what was going on. I only knew that in the last few minutes I'd become wretched and unhappy. . . and no doubt a bit scared. 'What did he say last night?'

'That's between him and me, darling. I two-timed him, didn't I?' (She faithfully employed the words of the cinema.) 'He was very angry. But it was worth it. I can't tell you. . .'

'Goodbye, you say?'

'He's taking a job in London. Going up tomorrow to stay with friends. And taking me with him because he doesn't trust me if I stay behind here. I've got to go. You won't understand, sweetheart. . . When things are sorted out, he's taking me off to Italy with him.' She threw her hands into the air, as if she was helpless to protest, as if life offered her no alternative.

We acted out the brief B-picture scene in the best traditions. The two cups of tea were left untouched on the stained tablecloth. Diana grasped my hand and placed it gently against her lips. She took my fingers and momentarily drew them into her mouth. Her parchment face, with those high cheek bones, twitched involuntarily. She looked different, harder even, without her make-up.

'Suppose I'll go on messing up my life. I've been doing it ever since I left school. It's been so nice. . . so different. . . to have you around. You know what I mean. Sherries with that famous Macmillan chap, proper dancing at the Manor Hotel. Here, do you really think he'll be the prime minister one day?'

I nodded. 'Something for you to remember.'

Wearily she got up from the table. 'Can't stay any longer. He doesn't know I've come. Wish me luck, sweetheart.'

She left me abruptly and walked out of the dirty little café, without looking back. In flat heels, the legs were unexceptional. I missed that hypnotic cheap perfume. I watched her until she was out of sight, on the other side of the steamed-up windows, silently pleading for one last glance. I wanted to hug her again: to thank her for my education, for the way she'd teased me and excited me, and left my emotions in a marvellous, disruptive tangle.

I knew I'd never see her again. Fade to black. Bring up grams. End of scene. Run credits.

'Snap out of it, you silly bugger. She was too old and experienced for you. Better out of that. And lucky not to have been carved up by that big Eye-tie.' My office colleague later that day had a point.

It would have helped my plaintive soul if my promotion to the reporters' room had brought some commensurate sense of fulfilment. But much of my time appeared to be spent writing prosaic paragraphs, monumentally un-newsworthy and better suited to a parish magazine. Occasionally I covered the courts, where the felons were for the most part no more than minor traffic offenders. Defendants and journalists, sharing the same small town, often knew each other. There was much nodding and shrugging or, when now and then there was evidence of discovered indecency in one of the public lavatories, blushing.

There was also the diversion of reporting my own case. I was caught one late winter's night, riding my cycle without a rear lamp. A shout of apprehension had been followed by the shadowy sight of a young constable emerging triumphantly from a side lane.

'Hold on, son. What d'you think you're doing without a light at the back?'

Son, indeed. And, worse than that, it was a young policeman I knew pretty well. At least that would be a let-off for me.

'Oh, it's you, Gordon. What's up, then? Rear light? Sorry about that – battery must be flat.' It was sounding a bit silly and phoney but, well, we'd played cricket against each other only back in August, and we often exchanged a 'Good morning' outside the courtroom.

'What's up, you say. The battery's bloody flat, all right. Got you, haven't I? What you got to say, then?' He was actually taking out his little notebook and through habit licking his minute lead pencil.

'Come on, Gordon,' I joked. 'Give me a hundred yards and see if you can catch me between here and Coker.'

Even as I said it, I could see he was in no mood to share my levity. The phlegmatic, unimaginative Gordon was topping up his tally for the month. In an atmosphere of strained embarrassment, he wrote down my name and address and told me eventually that I might be hearing from the court.

I persisted in the optimistic view that it was still a practical joke. I shouldn't have. The summons arrived in the post and my parents who in the way of many village people honoured the letter of the law and treated local bobbies with something approaching awe, were horrified that I should be in trouble. A court appearance clearly carried a stigma. It wasn't the kind of thing you liked the neighbours to hear about.

'Didn't you ask this policeman to let you off just this time – seeing that you knew him and might have a drink with him some time?' said my father, not averse to some mild corruption.

My appearance coincided with a day I was due to cover the court. I didn't tell anyone in the office. When my name was called, there was consternation and then general amusement among the reporters from the other papers, seated alongside me. I nervously threw them a smile and climbed out of the press bench and into the dock. I looked up at the magistrates and was reassured to find them smiling, too.

Not so the young constable, as he stood, tall, gaunt and humourless in a row of police officers, ready in case I should face up defiantly to the heinous crime and change my plea to Not Guilty.

The prosecuting solicitor glanced back over his shoulder at me before grinning. He liked to have a half with the reporters at the Half Moon on a Friday lunchtime. He gave the facts in a nice, racy manner, devoid of legal jargon. He told the magistrates how I'd been stopped when I displayed no rear light on my cycle. 'And the defendant, your worships, when questioned by the police officer, challenged him to catch him over one hundred yards!' He said it with a laughing lilt to the voice. But I still flushed. Surely, Gordon had recognised that was just a bit of intended badinage, certainly not meant for a notebook and a court of law. The magistrates enjoyed the spirit of the sporting challenge, waving away the formalities of the remaining token evidence.

'Have you anything you want to tell us, Mr – er – Fouracre?'

'No, thank you.' That sounded nice and polite as I listened to my faltering, unfamiliar voice wafting round the austere, varnish-smelling corners of the courtroom. But shouldn't I say something else? 'That. . . that hundred-yard business was just a bit of a joke. I wasn't trying to get away from the policeman. I'm. . . I'm sorry about the light but it was a cold night and I still had three miles to get home. My parents would have been getting anxious.'

That sentimental postscript made me feel self-conscious in the presence of my fellow scribes. Yet it seemed rather lame to apologise simply for a spent battery. Better to appeal to the paternal and maternal instincts of those homely confederates on the bench. Maybe they would be moved by the image of a shivering lad, who could have been their own, wanting only to get home to his family and a good coal fire.

The chairman, who ran an ironmonger's shop and possessed a compassionate Non-Conformist face, scratched his nose. 'Five shillings. Afraid we've got to fine you. Now you'd better go back and report the rest of the day's misdemeanours, hadn't you.' A nice man, I decided. I'd go to him in future for my cycle batteries.

My colleagues, rather admiringly I felt, made way for me to resume my seat on the press bench. Later, when it came to writing up the morning's cases, I impartially slipped in mine with the others. 'Matthew Edward Fouracre, of Verandah Cottage, East Coker, was fined five shillings for riding a bicycle without a rear light.' Just that. Right in the middle of a quarter-column of lighting offences, seven of which were brought on the initiative of the unsmiling, ever-vigilant Gordon.

Nothing was said in the office. I don't believe the sub-editors ever realised it was me.

But it was still a bad week for me. I thought again of Diana – I was rather more than five bob out of pocket.

NINE

For Whom The Bells Tolled

MR CHAPMAN, pink-cheeked and benevolent, was in a Friday morning frame of mind, relaxed and even jocular. He squeezed his head round the reporters' door and squinted through his rimless glasses. I was alone in the corner seat, the back page of the *Daily Herald* on my desk. There was a pencil impressively poised in my hand; in fact, I was engaged on my latest diversion to the more jejune aspects of my job, selecting five shilling-each-way cross doubles from the card at Thirsk. This recently acquired exercise in delusory self-aggrandizement was costing a pound a day. And to my astonishment I was modestly in profit since I had started my furtive calls on the local newsagent who doubled up as an illegal bookie's runner.

'Are you busy, young Matthew?'

'Just practising a bit of Pitman's, Mr Chapman – straight from the morning papers.'

He didn't put my smug, deceptive assurance to the test. But he evidently approved. 'That's what I like to hear. As I told you the other day, you're coming along nicely. Yes, very nicely. Let me see, wasn't that your report of St Michael's parochial church council meeting in today's paper?' I nodded just a little apprehensively. He went on: 'My good wife thought it was very well done. You got all the necessary names in. And spelt them correctly. Oh dear, there's nothing worse in the *Gazette* than a name spelt wrongly.'

And I knew he meant it. I believe that was his definitive yardstick for outstanding journalism. My report had run to all of three sticks, broken arbitrarily by the subs into two paragraphs. And yes, I could now remember that there had been a Mrs Chapman re-elected to the council. So Cherry wasn't a charcoal-grey-suited Wesleyan after all.

'We're getting a little more newsprint through these days. So perhaps, just occasionally mind you, there may be scope for you to come up with what in the profession is called a featured article. Do you know what that is?'

Of course I bloody did. Features were those longer pieces which you found on the leader pages of the *News Chron* and the *Mail*, with big bylines and sometimes a specially taken picture as well. I nodded again meekly.

'Featured articles are usually written by senior reporters. They are a little bit different. And I might consider one from you. Something maybe about the countryside. We're essentially a rural paper, you know. And you being a village boy.' I didn't really like the way he said that. His head withdrew and he was gone, tapping contentedly with his rolled umbrella as he descended the stairs.

I contemplated my line of four outsiders and an odds-on favourite from Thirsk, pocketed the potential fortune for later dispatch to my moonlighting newsagent and then, after no more than a minute's contemplation, typed a memo.

Journalistic ideas were never a problem for me, only the execution of them.

> TO MR CHAPMAN: Would you consider a feature article on campanology. My father is a ringer and he could arrange for me to sit in at a practice session. It is a growing hobby and I think many of our readers would be interested.

I was rather proud of 'campanology', a word I had never heard of before it came up at the reporters' last game of Hang the Man, when seemingly we had moved on from bodily functions and lascivious notions to matters ecclesiastical.

My memo was put neatly into an envelope and left on the assistant editor's desk. He ignored it for a month. Then, by felicitous timing, a handbell ringer turned up with all his musical impedimenta to address and entertain the Rotarians. He told them he sometimes rang the 40cwt tenor at Yeovil's parish church, too, and fascinated them by the juggling mathematics of going through the changes during a peal. Suddenly my idea was acceptable. 'Let me see, didn't you say you'd like to try to do something about bellringing? Why not. I can't promise it'll be quite good enough – but it's useful practice for you. Now don't forget, church towers are consecrated places. Behave yourself. And don't offend the vicar in any way.'

It had been, I suppose, something of a disappointment to my father that I had never shown any inclination to become a ringer myself. Our parish church was proud of its eight bells – tenor 13cwt, affiliation fee 10s 6d, according to the diocesan handbook – which offered near neighbours and distant hill dwellers inconsistent degrees of precision and mellifluence as a prelude to morning and evening service on Sundays. The pastime seemed to me far too intense and energy-consuming, especially after a teenage Saturday night of eagle-eyed foxtrotting and ostentatious drinking from pint mugs.

The assorted band rang on alternate Sundays. In between, my father supervised the chiming. He and his best man, Dick, wrapped bell ropes around each arm and strategically placed me in the centre of this improvised trio. That made five bells from three practitioners but the two adults had a wary regard for my sense of timing and coordination. It was the nearest I ever came to being a bellringer. Maybe, on reflection, my father opted for tact and didn't encourage me.

There was nothing fancy when it came to the chiming, no changes or anything like that. Just 1-2-3-4-5. It became quite a doddle after a time. You only swung the bell through a small arc – and when you jerked on the sally, the clapper would strike against the sound bow of the bell. I was apt to get quite blasé about it. 1-2-3-4-5. . . 1-23-4-5. . . 'Steady on, son, slow it down a bit'. . . 1-2-34-5. Or sometimes simply 1-2---4-5. No sign or sound from my No 3. I think I was tolerated. Worshippers, walking piously up the yew-lined church path, were known to look with some irritation towards the belfry window. Such wayward ringing practice, they felt, was out of place on a peaceful Sunday morning.

I asked if I could come along and watch at the next Tuesday practice session. It didn't seem necessary to add that I hoped to chronicle the experience for posterity. It was agreed and I took my seat in the wide window recess. My instructions were to keep quiet. My father, wise man, probably prayed that I was not formulating any plans to become a fulltime ringer.

The tower was well known to me. One of Dad's jobs was each night to bend double and wind the chimes, ensuring the quaint, cumbersome carillon would grind into action every three hours with a tune from *Ancient and Modern* rather like 'Underneath the Spreading Chestnut Tree'. The labour took nearly a quarter of an hour and needed regular pauses for breath. At times he left it to me. I would climb up the stone-worn spiral staircase, an oil lantern or flickering candle in my hand. On my way to the clockroom, I would invariably stop to look in the belfry. There was always something especially appealing about that circle of dangling sallies. I used to place the

lantern on the table and sit for a few minutes on the wooden bench.
The ringers' changes were neatly printed on a hanging board, like
figures on a football coupon.

When I went out of the belfry I remembered unfailingly to lock
the door. After that, I'd go up to wind the chimes and the clock. As
I turned the handle there was much cranking of antiquated mecha-
nism and squeaking of the rope, like you get on a fisherman's line,
as it coiled itself into its new position. The flame from the lantern
would flicker eerily across the crumbling plaster of the walls. But boys
of seventeen or eighteen saw little fear.

The Tuesday practice night for the ringers lasted for about two
hours, an arrangement leaving ample time for voracious thirsts to
be quenched after an eager step down through the Paddock walk to
the New Inn. I looked round the belfry at the men, some of whom
had come straight from work. Their shirt sleeves were already rolled
high to reveal their sturdy forearms. They were physical in the way
only countrymen are – and they appeared thirsty even before they
had started.

They were all there: old Teddy, with his lugubrious expression
and thick bushy moustache that made him look a bit like Stalin. . .
Jack, who doctored the cats and swept the chimneys. . . Gilby, who
never remembered to put in his false teeth, and was said to leave them
permanently in a tea cup on the kitchen table. . . Wicker, warm-
hearted and cheeky, one who never allowed the stifling ambience
of holy ground to ruin a good story. . .

Only seven had turned up, so they settled for six bells. 'Just a bit
of simple Stedman,' said the captain, Teddy, indistinctly through
his drooping Bolshevik moustache. They took up their places in a
circle round the table, from which two paraffin lanterns threw a cosy
warm glow round the little room. Automatically they looped the end
of the rope in their hands back onto the sally. They weren't talking
any longer. Village men, who all week used their hands to saw wood
at the mill, to turn the clay soil ready for the winter frosts, to lay
cement paths, were now about to use their heads in an exercise of
unrelieved concentration. If they lapsed and their strike went out
of sequence, they knew Teddy would, from his glance of withering
reprimand, be sentencing them to the Salt Mines.

The ringers were comically assorted in build. They were tall and
squat, with their bulging biceps and home-knitted pullovers. One,
back from the Navy, had incongruous tattoos on his hairy arms. There
were cloth caps stuffed in trouser pockets. Wicker had a stubbed-out

cigarette still behind his ear. Dick dared to break the silence. 'Must get somebody to have a look at No 5, Teddy. There's a bit of a crack coming in the crown. Frank and me spotted it when we was up there doing some oiling. Pity, that. She's a lovely bell.'

As I quickly discovered, the bells – like ships – assumed an air of femininity. They were much loved by their ringers; they had personalities of their own. Dick's comment stalled the start of the practice, as if an excuse had been found to put off the mental processes ahead. It led to a new burst of conversation. 'Old Bert at Hardington done a Plain Bob Minor at Merriott t'other day. Two hours and a half. Bit of a sweat near the end – one of 'em nearly lost his way.' An esoteric and mathematical theory about Grandsire Triples, incomprehensible to the other six, was cut short as Teddy, stocky and officious, took a renewed grip on his sally. 'Le's be hearing from thee, then. Everybody ready?. . . Treble away!'

The treble rope was tugged and then went bounding up through the aperture in the ceiling. And, in more or less strict rotation, five more ropes followed the same route – before returning down through the ceiling, to be grabbed by waiting hands. Six red-and-green sallies darting up and down: and suddenly the whole belfry throbbing with the magnified sound of bells right above us.

This small room was rocking to the vibrations and the body heat. It was all hairy arms, flapping shirtsleeves, flailing ropes that soared out of sight and, one after the other, reappeared again, grunts, rattling of coins in back pockets, pleasant whiffs of manly sweat and the amber flame from two lanterns which flickered boldly and then receded in the varying currents of corporate muscle. All the time, the bell ropes squeaked on the woodwork as they made their way through the hole in the ceiling.

Our band of parish ringers had been taught not to follow with their eyes the frantic course, up and down, of the sallies. They looked straight ahead, comically serious in the manner of deadpan straight men on the halls. The captain would intermittently break the human stillness with a laconic 2-1-4-3-6-5. . . 2-4-1-6-3-5-. . . 4-2-6-1-5-3. And then they eventually returned to a straight run, listening for the Stalinist grunt of finality that told them it was time to stop.

One of the middle bells showed a reluctance to do so and offered a whimpering strike twice more. Teddy looked in eloquent silence towards the culprit. The belfry remained silent almost without sound for twenty seconds or so, save for some heavy breathing and the rustle

of still restless ropes. Then came the surge of relief and revived conversation. 'You'm pullin' nice and steady on her tonight, Herb.'. . .
'There bain't a better tenor in the diocese, Gilby. She'm going like
a beauty.' And then a mild reprimand for one of the younger ringers.
'We do keep telling 'ee tis knack – not bloody brute force.' The odd slip
of the tongue was inevitable when it came to a group of uninhibited
villagers flexing their muscles. They just hoped the occasional exple-
tive could be stifled on the nights the parson looked in.

There was a ten-minute break. One or two put their coats over
their shoulders, went downstairs and out in the moonlight, sitting on
a large, leaning table-like tombstone for their obligatory fag. Another
moved a few steps up the spiral stairway, out of Teddy's sight, for a
Woodbine. He didn't reckon God would object.

The rest sat round the belfry to discuss a parochial topic, hardly
suited to a place of worship, which had grown in avid interest since
the *Gazette* had appeared on the previous Friday. 'Surprised they
printed it, son,' someone said to me, as it dawned on him that
I worked there. I was reasonably well briefed and replied with as
much authenticity as a mere teenager can muster: 'All done through
her solicitor. So nothing really to stop her. She had to pay for it, of
course. Threepence a word.'

The offending, or rather titillating, paragraph had preceded the
rest of Coker's racy news of sale stallholders and whist-drive winners.
It was printed in 5-point italic, denoting that it was an advertisement.
And it told the readers of our moderately pious parish that a specific
young lady, well known to all of us, wanted it to be firmly understood
that she jolly well wasn't pregnant and that she was ready to take legal
action against anyone who chose to perpetuate the rumour. Not quite
in those words – but that was the gist.

Rumour? I certainly hadn't heard it before. There had been a
few buns illicitly baked in Coker's ovens over the years, of course;
plenty of furtive flings, even on occasions no doubt transcending
the social barriers in the best D.H. Lawrence traditions. Long
before notions of journalism entered my head, I had been a
ready recipient of carnal gossip. As a schoolboy, I had been privy
through eavesdropping prowess to whispered tales of marvellous,
lascivious wartime alliances. At times my eyeballs threatened to
bounce clean out of their sockets at the sight, not always cloaked
in shadowy discretion, of erotic dalliances in the backyard of the
pub, just across the road from my cottage. But here was one rumour
I had missed completely. I felt an instant failure, even though the

girl had now gone to pains to deny that her tummy was beginning to bulge.

'Only bringing notice to it, she were.'

'Maybe she bin down to see old Mrs Gregory. And got it done away wi'. Now she's saying it ain't never happened,' laughed another of the ringers.

I knew all about Mrs Gregory. She was renowned for her herbal remedies – for warts, boils and piles. They did say, out of the corner of the mouth, that she was also pretty proficient when it came to syringes and a bottle of Dettol. She kept a seed shop in the town. But she didn't seem to sell many seeds. Whenever I walked past her dust-laden shop window, I saw the same faded packets of asters. She must have had, some of the lads in the office suggested darkly, another source of income.

All I can say is that she was never prosecuted. 'Old Maggie Gregory. . . ah, she were a good friend to half the girls in Yeovil through two world wars. She knowed what to do. Nothing never went wrong. That's why they didn't never catch up with her.' The ringers exchanged various possible reasons for the unusual advertisement. Everyone seemed to agree she was among the less promiscuous girls in the village. No-one was ever able to work out what possessed her with such Freudian zeal to make public a slender, even self-created rumour.

Now it was time to resume the ringing. Work-stained, well-worn coats were hooked back onto the belfry pegs. The lantern wick was turned up a fraction. Two more ringers, who had arrived late, now took their turn. It was still to be six bells only. 'Treble away!' And the rustle of human activity and the vibrations started all over again.

I pulled out my lined reporter's notebook and jotted down a few impressions. They weren't necessarily the kind, I accept on reflection, that my journalistic elders would have considered worthy of record. Wicker, now sitting in the window seat, was doing his Littlewoods, I noted. My eyes circled the room as the ringers heaved and stretched and went up on their toes. I noticed the heavily darned socks, and shirts stitched by painstaking wives who had noticed the first signs of tears at the seams. I noticed, too, the three half-pint bottles of Bruttons, aligned like sentries on the bench, ready for tombstone consumption at the end of the evening's session. And above all, I was fascinated by the initial range of Stedman changes on the varnished board. How many permutations could there possibly be? I really could see the mathematical appeal for Mr Sherman and Mr Zetter and the rest of them.

My work was more or less done. I'd absorbed the atmosphere of the cosy little belfry: and those hairy forearms that pumped away in the pursuit of disciplined rotation and music-making. It was nearly half past eight and there were other things on my mind. The most pressing was a show-business audition at the Assembly Rooms in Yeovil at nine o'clock.

The audition was for would-be Carroll Levis Discoveries. 'Report promptly at nine – with your music,' the grubby little buff note, badly typed, had said. 'Please be on time as we have many more auditions to go threw during the evening.'

I had seen the advert in the *Gazette*, inviting potential radio stars to apply for a place on Mr Levis's famous show. His face grinned down at us from the corner of the ad – a fat, jolly face, topped by sleekly parted fair hair. He could have been inviting us to a revival-ist meeting. 'Step on the stairway to success,' said the notice in the *Gazette*. 'I'm looking for the great artistes of tomorrow.'

Lyric-writing was my latest whim. I churned out caustic couplets as I ate mother's jam sandwiches in my lunch break. At home, pre-ferably when mother was out of the way, I tried out my personalised wit, still substantially culled from the beloved style of prewar inti-mate revue and the languid verbal counterpoint of the Western Brothers.

Our proudest domestic possession was a dark wood upright piano, for which my parents had nobly saved before providing me with the money for my first lessons as a six-year-old, seven and sixpence a quarter. There was much parental joy when I passed my prelimi-nary and first-grade exam. After that, I gave my forbearing tutor mounting discouragement as I insisted on introducing an element of syncopation, in the way of that stubby-fingered wizard, my idol Stan Russell, when it came to some simple Handel. I gave up lessons, never progressing technically from that point, but acquiring a facil-ity to play a maximum of three numbers, including 'In The Mood', with Naafi-nurtured ferocity and daydream aplomb. When the lyrics later arrived, scribbled on scraps of paper, I set them to plagiarized segments of familiar music. The piano was placed alongside the wall, and on the roughly hewn stone floor so uneven that a straw mat wore out in three months. When I thumped my strident chords, fancifully looking over my shoulder at the dinner-jacketed dancers on the hotel dance floor, the piano in reality rocked alarmingly on its castors.

My lyrics were written for two voices, with us alternating over the third-line rhyming joke which was inclined to be mildly risqué. Dick was my singing partner. We'd gone to school together and he knew most of the tunes that I had plagiarized. Dick had a nice church-choir tenor emerging. He also possessed invaluable twin facilities – he could keep in tune and enunciate quite beautifully. The pair of us took limited bookings at some of the more coveted alhambras of the neighbourhood, like the Legion Hall, Tintinhull. We didn't charge. That seemed to be getting above yourself.

Dick, although busy studying for his first accountancy exams, had been primed about the audition. We would do our current big hit, 'Work, work, nothing but work. . .' We were rather proud of our ad-lib harmonising and the clever little musical and vocal interjections between the lines. If the occasional reference was just a little saucy, well we were still surprised that our fair-minded vicar murmured his disapproval after the last boys' club concert in the village hall. I had developed a mannered cough of aristocratic wholesomeness after delivering a risqué line. Dick's voice was so angelic that the naughty nuance rapidly assumed respectability.

During the break back at the belfry, I had implied that I would have to leave long before the end. Now, with the ringers intent on their football-pool Stedman – could Wicker really have been working out the next logical move for the treble instead of the prospects for White Hart Lane? – I reckoned they would be oblivious to my stealthy departure. I slipped out, closing the door behind me.

I had left my three-speed alongside the almshouses at the bottom of the church path. It never took me more than twenty minutes cycling to the centre of Yeovil, helped by the speedy descent of Hendford Hill. I hummed my topical lyrics as I pedalled and thought of the Western Brothers, though in truth Dick and I sang with the unmistakable burr of our Coker roots rather than with the affectedly indolent drawl of the late-night, smoky Savoy.

There were comings and goings at the Assembly Rooms. Most of the singers coming out, sheet music under their arms, looked as if they belonged to the light operatic societies of Yeovil, Crewkerne, Chard and Ilminster. I walked into the main hall and someone was singing 'Bless This House'.

Dick was already there, sitting in a converted cinema seat, his head in a book on company law. He didn't look nervous, nor particularly interested.

A little man, cigarette stuck to his lips, came up. He had an East End accent and a fast delivery. He didn't seem to be listening to the singer. 'Here for the audition, are you? Running late. Always the bloody same. Name?'

'Er – Fouracre and Newton. Two voices, one piano.'

'Oh, double act. Where's your partner?'

I pointed to Dick, reading a dreary tome with small type and no pictures.

'That's him, is it. Saw him come in. Didn't think he was interested. Just waiting to clear the chairs away at the end.'

The little man's enthusiasm was waning by the minute. I felt it was time for a little self-projection. 'We do songs at the piano. Dick's got a really nice voice.'

'Thank God, you're a bit different, son. Just listen to that up there. On my life, it's the fifth bloody time we've had "Bless This House" tonight. And each one worse than the one before.'

'When are we on?' It was surprising, I found, how quickly you got into the phraseology of showbiz.

'Sit down and wait. Three or four more before you. Keep it short, remember. Four minutes, something like that. That'll be enough for me to tell. You'll be using the grand up on the stage. We've got some sort of mike wired up for you as well. Hope it works. Remember to speak up.'

I went over and sat with Dick. 'Isn't he here, then?'

'Who?'

'This Carroll Levis bloke.'

Dick had assimilated the set-up before getting down to his textbook. 'No, only that chap you were talking to, and a girl who's making some notes.'

I told Dick I'd written three additional verses but he would be able to read them without any trouble if he stayed close to my shoulder. The idea was for me to place my assorted sheets of bedraggled lyrics on the music rest and for my partner, blessed with excellent eyesight, surreptitiously to read them between worldly grins at his audience. I liked to amend my lyrics for the occasion. This time I'd cheekily penned a verse about Mr Levis making his best discovery of all when he got back to his hotel after the show. Maybe it was just as well he hadn't bothered to come along for the audition.

134

Before it was our turn, there were two brothers who played the piano accordion and rather cleverly switched to the other's keyboard for the final chorus of *Orpheus in the Underworld*. I was much impressed and applauded without thinking. No-one else did. Someone did a Marie Lloyd impression (she had a North Country voice and I thought it was meant to be Tessie O'Shea) and then came, to our surprise, a sand dancer who seemed unaware that the audition was supposed to be for radio. He took ages sprinkling the stage with sand and then danced 'Bye Bye Blackbird' completely out of time to his wife's piano playing.

The little man was getting very impatient. 'Right, now. Let's get a move on, for Gawd's sake. Fouracre & Newton.' Our audience was down to this bloke and his apathetic secretary, as well as half a dozen critical and curious onlookers, most of whom were still waiting for their turn to go on.

Dick and I climbed up onto the stage. I stuck two loose leaves from my reporter's notebook on the music rest and took my seat. Dick, the intuitive professional, stood behind me, right arm on my right shoulder. At the same time he was checking whether he could read the three new verses.

But we might as well have been singing to bodies on a mortuary slab. The jokes went without response. Dick's splendid tenor twirls were unappreciated. We might have been warbling the repetitive verbiage on a seed catalogue. I imagine we did the arbitrary four minutes. There was a second song, 'The Mannequin Parade', folded in my inside pocket, just in case we were asked for an encore. We weren't.

'OK. . . next!' He didn't even say thanks.

A paper-tearer climbed onto the stage as we were coming down.

Dick went to collect his book on company law from the converted cinema seat and as we walked towards the door, in slightly irritated anticlimactic silence, the little man's secretary came after us. She had a death-mask complexion and a breath that compounded the butts of a day's supply of cheap fags, taken without food in a fusty, confined space. But she surprised us with a lovely smile that transcended the vacuous exterior.

'Don't get too depressed. Only an audition, you know. Bernie doesn't say much at the time but he takes it all in. You could be hearing from us again. Can't promise.' We thanked her.

The little East Ender must have been reading the girl's lips. He suddenly shouted across the hall. 'And if you do hear from me again, make sure you cut out that reference to Carroll. Cheeky sods!'

Dick and I cycled home together, by way of the Chelsea Tea Rooms (more popular for their suppers) for Welsh rabbit and a cup of coffee. He lived on the main road on the outskirts of West Coker, three miles from my home. We'd shared elementary school, grammar school and now a Carroll Levis audition. There was always much to talk and gossip about. We talked and roared with laughter for more than an hour. And then a strange thing happened.

We heard church bells. I looked at my wristwatch in the moonlight and saw that it was nearly midnight. The tone of the bells was unmistakable. It was the parish bells at St Michael's, the tower I'd left earlier in the evening.

At once we came to the conclusion that the only reason the church bells could be ringing at that hour was in celebration. But for what? The bells had swung jubilantly at all hours when we won the war. Had another war now been won on some distant hillside of the globe. We could think of none. Maybe East Coker had just produced a new offspring of noble blood? I had heard of no rumours of imminent visits from doctors and midwives at the Tudor courthouse. Yet what stupendous deed might now have been considered worthy of recalling thirsty ringers from the New Inn? I listened again: all eight bells were mellifluously in motion. The stilled countryside of South Somerset was alive to the incongruously timed music of St Michael's.

And then the bells stopped. The Western Brothers returned to the sophisticated world of waspish words. We heard midnight strike – and then one o'clock. The bells were forgotten and I prepared for my cycle ride home. Then, with bizarre suddenness, East Coker's belfry burst into sound yet again.

'What's going on down there?' asked Dick. 'Something splendid must have happened.' He tilted his head to listen, as if expecting a dozen other church towers to join in an exultant chorus. 'Perhaps we ought to come into the house and see if there's anything on the wireless. There may be a special news bulletin or something.'

We went in and Dick put the set on the table. There was much crackling, positively no voices, as he twiddled the knob from end to end. 'Strange, that. . .' We both agreed something historic had happened. Ah well, I'd simply have to go home to my village to find out.

On the ride home, my curiosity was increasing. Perhaps the ringing would go on all through the night. For heaven's sake, they'd still been pulling at twenty past one. I must surely go up to the tower again: the perfect, dramatic way of rounding off my article for the *Gazette*.

Why weren't the other parishes joining in the celebrations, though? I pulled up, turned off my front light and listened. There wasn't a sound. East Coker, too, was at sleep, oblivious to what was going on.

Then I saw two cycle lights coming towards me, probably a hundred yards or more off. The voices were loud and decidedly tetchy. I recognised them even in the darkness; they belonged to two of the ringers.

'The silly bugger. What made him lock the belfry door?'

'I don't know what the missus is going to say. Half past bloody one – and we've been ringing for most of the soddin' night.'

'And no-one took a blind bit of notice. Might've bin starvin' to bloody death.'

By this time the horror of what had happened had dawned on me. I swiftly dragged my bike and myself deep into the shadows at the side of the road. The ringers cycled past, their front lights darting along the hedgerows with every slight movement of the handlebars. Their voices refused to die.

'Why the hell didn't summun hure us as they comed out of the pub? They must've knowed summit were up. We don't never ring that late when there's beer to be drunk.'

'Could've bin there all bloody night. And the laughin' stock of the village. All very well fer Teddy to say we 'ad to keep going till the passon hured us.'

The voices were fading away. 'Why didn't 'ee think of it before, Albert?'

I slunk home. I knew by now exactly what I had done. For years, when my father had asked me to wind the chimes, he had said: 'And whatever you do, don't forget to lock the tower when you come down.'

My father was waiting, rather uneasily pulling on his moustache. Mother had made him a big cup of cocoa and I noticed he had dropped a little medicinal whisky in the top. I got in first, blurting out: 'But Dad, you told me so often to lock the door that this time I did it without thinking. Don't say anything. I know it's terrible. I'll write a letter of apology to all the ringers.'

When Dad had mellowed sufficiently, I dared to ask how the ringers had eventually made their escape. 'We let Albert out through the window on a bell rope. It was his idea. Suppose we should have thought of it earlier.'

Much chastened, I went up to my bedroom and wrote my letter of fawning apology to the captain of the bellringers. I also decided, more pragmatically, to send up a big bottle of Scotch for Sunday morning consumption before, or more likely instead of, matins. In the meantime, it seemed tactful for me to stay as far away from St Michael's as possible for the rest of the week.

There followed the inevitable dilemma, of course. Surely it was too good a story to ignore. RINGERS LOCKED IN TOWER ALL NIGHT. . . RINGERS SHIN DOWN A BELL ROPE TO FREEDOM. . . I slept fitfully on that one.

My mother promised to deliver the letter of apology, while I cycled in spineless haste to Yeovil, yellow oilskin lending anonymity to my cowardice.

The assistant editor pre-empted my agonised decision-making, as parochial well-being battled it out with journalistic instinct. He stopped me in the corridor. 'I've been thinking about that idea you had for a little feature article on ringers, young Matthew. I don't think it's quite strong enough. . . perhaps a trifle too technical. Now I'm a churchgoing person myself, as you may well know, but I don't feel very much of interest happens in the belfry. Do you?'

'No, Mr Chapman,' I lied.

'Not that I want to discourage you. Leave it for a few weeks and then try again. With perhaps a slightly better subject next time?'

On the Monday there was a note waiting for me at home, from the captain of the ringers. 'Thanks for your note, son. You gave us all a bit of a scare but we have now had time to have a laugh about it. Don't do it again, though. The ringers asked me to thank you for the whisky. We all had a drop out round the back but I don't think you had better tell the vicar. Now Albert has shown us the way, we aren't too worried about getting locked in again.'

I also had a note on the Tuesday, through the post. It was from Bernie, the little man who ran the Levis auditions. The spelling wasn't much better than before:

'Just to tell you I quite liked the act, two voices one piano and I shall be putting you and your partner on in our reginal heets next month. The best three will be considered for Carroll Levis's discoveries program on the radio or a new road show of his but a word of advise their will be an audience next time so I suggest the pair of you smarten yourself up and lern your words so that you dont need to read them off a piece of scrappy paper. Good luck yours in showbusiness. . . Bernie Silvers'

I thought of writing a song about a band of bellringers, generously prepared to pass on a few tricks to restless Dartmoor prisoners anxious to change their place of residence. But Dick was coming up to his accountancy exams and I preferred the ambience of Tintinhull's Legion Hall. We didn't go on to the heats.

TEN

Cup Ecstasy

EARLY AFTERNOON was Rowly's best time. He had sunk his statutory three pints of Worthy during his lunch break. Now he was mellow and talkative. His cistern-battered nose was shining with the remnants of bar-room perspiration. He was ready to banter and belch good-humouredly -- and condense conscientiously compiled village football reports, submitted in their best handwriting by club officials, with summary jocularity.

'Just look at this lot,' he'd say to no-one in particular, with extravagant shaking of the head. 'They lost 7-1 and, according to this bloke, they still served up some of their neatest football of the season so far.' He would ponder such partial analysis. 'And tomorrow, you bloody bet, I'll get a completely different report from the other team's chairman. Who do you believe? Can't be the glowing one about the poor sods who've let in seven.'

Rowly would offer these soliloquies in the immediate post-lunch period. That was when he always subjected his colleagues to philosophical asides on the current state of British journalism. It made a change from the early-morning political bile. Yet the thing about Rowly was that, despite his incessant boozing and bigotry, we all liked him.

It was about half past two when he came in looking for me. When he was at peace with the world and the shoulder-chips weren't showing, he would walk distinctively with his hands deep in his trouser pockets and with a marked swagger of the shoulders.

'What's your rugby like, Matt?'

'Played it at school.'

'Not one of those soccer nancies, then. Better game altogether, rugby.'

Emboldened by his bonhomie, I asked with some presumption: 'Are you looking for someone to cover Yeovil this season?'

'Had it in mind. There must be a few bob in it for you – as long as you don't tell Cherry. Haven't had any decent rugby coverage in the paper since the war was over. And the treasurer drinks in my pub. He's always on about it.'

As there was absolutely no prospect of extra wages in working for the *Gazette* on a Saturday afternoon, the inducement of those 'few extra bob' – by looking after the home Yeovil matches for other papers – seemed like a most agreeable bonus.

'I wouldn't mind giving it a go.'

Rowly contemplated his own needs. 'I don't think I'd want too much. Just a short match report, and a bit about team changes for the next fixture. But for Christ's sake, don't get the score wrong.'

As bad as Cherry, I thought.

Overnight, my weekly earnings doubled from thirty bob. The *Sunday Dispatch*, *Sunday Express* and *Empire News* all wanted a hundred words on Yeovil's first team games. The senior reporter from another paper, who was the monopolistic correspondent for the Londons, promised me seven-and-sixpence from each one. I didn't always see it. But by my hitherto impecunious standards, I was now an emerging 'freelance' of substantial means. There were also ordered phone reports to be done for the three local evening papers' sports editions – at five shillings a time. I made an instant resolve to increase my housekeeping allowance to my mother, from ten to fifteen shillings a week.

The rugby club appeared delighted that they were at last to get some additional publicity. There was a corporate team vanity that revealed itself when the club earned a mention in a national paper – and the try scorers sheepishly glowed when they saw their names in print. It was part of the undoubted charm of unsophisticated smalltown life in the late Forties.

Yeovil in those days hadn't a ground of their own. They paid for a pitch on the recreation ground and changed in the nearby grammar school. I watched the games from an exposed, rain-lashed touchline and often at the end felt more in need of a shower than the players. At half time I would run down to a pub to phone my copy; a considerate licensee used to leave his back door on the jar. Within a week or so, I overcame my self-consciousness of talking to the players and confirming the try-scorers as they squatted on the school lockers, steam rising from their muscular, recently showered and eminently well-hung naked bodies.

The fixture secretary was apparently delegated to look after my journalistic needs. He was the assistant manager of one of the big banks in the town. He was much impressed that I had early-evening calls to make to Fleet Street. 'You must make them from the bank. The office will be private – and warm.' I used to ring the security bell and he would let me in. Banks on Saturday evenings are strangely empty places. The assistant manager, without the necessary authority of Head Office I felt, would sit me on a high stool amid the closed ledgers. And as I inhaled the affluent tang of freshly minted coinage, I'd make my reverse-charge calls to the *Dispatch, Express* and *Empire News*. He would stand at a discreet distance, nodding in quiet approval as I found my excuse to give Yeovil the praise they rarely deserved.

On Saturday afternoons I would walk, or more often run, up and down the line alongside the touch-judge of the home club. He offered the players much noisy advice which they seemed never to hear. He found it hard to obscure his bias. He blithely ignored the fact that the home winger's feet were half a yard into touch, if he was hell-bent for the line at the time.

Though no-one was ever sent off or seldom even rebuked by the referee, dreadful physical acts of aggression went on. Yeovil's skipper, a Devonian with the well-modulated voice that befitted an insurance executive, used his fists every week with quite villainous intent. It was the first real manifestation of schizophrenia I had come across. He would come off at the end, lips and cheeks bleeding profusely – as were invariably those of his opposite number in the front row – and applaud the other side off the field with an unbridled sense of gentlemanly etiquette and enthusiasm. 'Grand game,' he would say as he shook the hand of the opposing captain.

The home club also had an Irish full back, who had the good looks of an especially well-fed James Mason. His Guinness-laden tummy bulged over his shorts. He was in the side for his kicking, not much else. He never missed a long touch and rarely a conversion. Any penalty from the vicinity of the halfway line gave James Mason a real chance. He would teeter interminably on the toes of his big, black boots, stomach wobbling like Neapolitan blancmange, as he steadied himself for the kick. His penalties triumphed in inverse proportion to his tackles. I can't in honesty ever remember him tackling his man. He would have done so, no doubt, if he could ever have got within two yards of his marauding opponent. Every week James Mason's name was in the paper for his two conversions and three penalty goals. It didn't seem quite fair.

When Yeovil's senior side were playing away, I would cover the 'A' XV. The standard of rugby at that level was inclined to be as wayward and dire as the organisational pretensions. But the local sports papers, the Pink 'Un and the Green 'Un, still wanted reports of the 'A' matches for their Saturday night pages.

Team selection was flexible and habitually delayed. One or two of the better players would be commandeered without compunction on the Saturday morning by the first team. There was much cursing and pleading as harassed officials struggled to find fifteen players to make up the 'A' side. Positions on the field were only of nominal value. Big, overweight second-row forwards were momentarily flattered to discover they were playing as centre threequarters.

When it came to the visit of Wiveliscombe 'A', the home team could still only call on twelve players at ten to three. 'Bit of trouble with one of the goalposts,' the visitors were told. 'Sorry about it – but we may have to kick off at quarter past or just after.'

'Robbo', the team secretary who had not travelled with the first team as touch-judge, was beside himself. He was frantically running round, in permutations of anger, bewilderment and resignation, as he searched vainly for last-minute replacements. 'This is the last year I'm doing the job,' he kept repeating. 'All the cards went out on time – and we're still three short. Nothing short of a disgrace. Wait till I get to the meeting on Monday night.'

The secretary looked out of the window of the poky dressing room on the recreation ground itself, designated to the 'A' team. There appeared to be just three spectators waiting for the indeterminate kick-off. Two of them were players' girl friends. The third was a bespectacled young man with a dog on a lead. It transpired later that he did the walk most Saturday afternoons, in expectations of a hockey match on one of the adjoining pitches.

Robbo turned to me. 'Get stripped off!' The order, barked out by a man with glazed eyes, shocked me. I'd last played, badly, as a fifth former. Outside the dressing room the rain was now slanting down and the loyal girls on the touchline had their umbrellas up. My own raincoat was turned up high and protectively at the collar. He repeated his command of despair. 'You've played before, haven't you – what's the matter? There's a spare pair of boots in the skip. Size won't be a problem – the boots are so big they'll fit every bugger in Yeovil.'

The eyes of the overworked secretary looked even more wild and deranged. He pressed them close to my face. 'Listen, if we go out onto the field with twelve perishing players, it's an insult to Wivvy.

It'll get back and we'll lose the first team fixture with them as well. So get that mac off.' I could see that through the faltering words of an unbalanced man he was being serious about my need to play.

'But I can't, Robbo. I'm doing a report of the match at half time.'

'I'll do it.' And he threw me a chocolate and sky blue-hooped shirt. 'What's your best position?'

'Front row.' It was where I played with a minimum of physical effort or even interest in the proceedings during futile, meandering form matches at school. Even as I said it now, I knew it was a monumental mistake. I thought again of the first-team skipper, himself a prop forward, and all his villainous activities in that ghastly tunnel of sweat and bent, evil bodies.

Wild Robbo pencilled my name into his book and scuttled out into the driving rain. With mounting panic, I pulled off my raincoat, sports coat, thick cotton shirt and winter vest. The navy blue shorts left for me were caked with mud from a previous fixture. I ascertained that no-one was looking as I slipped down my grey trousers and then underpants. The shorts were tight at the crutch. There were no spare socks so I kept on my own which came just above my ankles. Last-minute changing was going on all around me. There wasn't too much conversation – probably too many strangers in the side.

Robbo returned with the spectacled young man from the touchline. He had an expression of mild triumph. 'This young gent here. . . Vincent, is it?. . . Vincent's going to help us out. Just to make up the numbers a bit. We can stick him out on the wing.' The glasses were the thickest I had ever seen; the chances of him running in the right direction without them must be slim, I concluded. Robbo was now leading the dog. 'Don't worry about him, Vincent. I'll tie him to one of the flags – he can watch you all the afternoon.'

The secretary went on to address the rest of the team. 'Bloody shambles and you won't find me doing this job when it comes to the annual meeting. But we're up to fourteen. We can at least give 'em a game.'

He peered round the little dressing room, assuming the role of skipper as well as team secretary. 'Johnny had better lead the scrum. Em – no, he's about the only one who can take a clean pass. Johnny, you'd better switch to stand-off.' The autocratic tactical manoeuvring met with tacit agreement.

We took the field at twenty past three: to play with only seven forwards and a lock who would be theoretically poised to take any stray pass that came his way from a scrum-half who clearly wasn't going to have much say in what would be going on that afternoon. I was in the front row.

Johnny had a quick word with us. He'd once played for Somerset Police and knew a murky thing or two. He surveyed the pathetic array of rugby-playing raw material that Robbo had somehow dredged up for him. Maybe out of a sense of sympathy for me, he said: 'Wivvy can be dirty sods – they may be out to get you in the first five minutes.'

Prophetic words, more or less: it only took two minutes. The first time there was a knock-on, the front row linked arms and immediately lurched into combat with the opposing trio. I shuddered at the sheer ferocity of the motion, privately marvelling that our heads didn't collide with sickening thuds. We waited for the ball to come in, and to my horror and disbelief a thick, insensitive fist closed with the grip of a vice around my more private parts. I let out a squeal of excruciating pain. My eyes watered.

Shamed into explanation, I yelled. 'Someone's got me by the curlies.' It seemed to me that the long, dastardly arm was snaking out from the nefarious depths of Wivvy's second row. I assumed the deviant ploy would earn a prompt rebuke and perhaps a penalty. The only reaction I was conscious of was the gruff, unfeeling laughter of eight men shoving against us.

Our scrum-half, a relatively gentle soul who worked in the probation office, paused as he was about to release the ball. A fellow forward, from somewhere behind my left buttock, gave me practical advice. 'Well, grab him by the balls as well!'

My head was in confusion. Was this club rugby, the game of gentlemen? Was there not a better way for me to gain an insight into the finer points? The match had barely started and here I was being encouraged to take drastic, uncharacteristic action, in the region of the genitals, that would be the grounds for criminal indecency between consenting males during the rest of the week.

Over the forty minutes of the first half there were many line-outs and hardly any open rugby football. We took to booting the ball anything up to a hundred yards, into touch and way across the expansive recreation ground, whenever we had the chance. There was no spare ball and the blissful delay in play came as relief to the whole of our team. I stayed down as long as I could after the scrums but still felt exhausted. All the time I thought I was going to vomit. We were 38-nil down at the interval.

For the last five minutes of the half, my mind had been diverted to imminent journalistic commitments. When the whistle went, I hobbled to the line in search of Robbo. 'Sorry, son, no time to do your reports. It'll be all right – give 'em twice as much at the end.' It exemplified layman logic when it came to my professional discipline of deadlines. I might be a reluctant rugby player with weary limbs and tender testicles but a sense of loyalty to my profession took precedence.

I staggered up to the Wiveliscombe touch-judge and discovered that he had kept a record of his team's try-scorers and conversion-takers. He blinked at my request to lend me his list. 'Got to put it over for the papers. Might turn into a record score for your club,' I said with suspect allegiance to my own colours. The rain was streaming down my muddy face and my shorts were sticking to my bruised thighs. But I clutched his list gratefully and, to the consternation of Robbo, set off for the pub. 'I'll be back,' I called with none too much conviction.

I kicked off my sodden king-sized boots and left them at the back door, on the jar for me as usual. Then, still out of breath, I ad-libbed my three reports. Yeovil 'A' didn't get much of a mention. It was hard to justify one in just a hundred words when they had done absolutely nothing of note or merit. I tried to give a suggestion of narrative when it came to Wivvy's nine tries; I may have got the sequence wrong, certainly in my fictitious build-up to each gem of a touch-down. I finished my last account of open rugby at its purest – and saw a pool of water, from my dripping clothes, on the pub's tiled floor. That was no way to treat kindly hosts. I peeled off my shirt and used it as a floor cloth. Then, appalled by my necessary improvisations, I pulled the chocolate and sky blue garment, colours by now becoming indistinguishable, over my head again.

My dishevelled form arrived back at the pitch with twenty minutes left. Yeovil were showing some laudable resistance. They were trailing 52-nil. There was a frosty glare from Robbo. 'Johnny's gone into the pack to give it some weight. Tuck yourself into the back row, son. And for heaven's sake, do a bit of shoving.'

We all lost count of the score by the end but I knew I'd be able to check again with the Wivvy touch-judge. His earlier list was safely tucked deep down the side of my right boot. The teams came off the field and did the obligatory mutual three-cheers. It was rather muted.

'Sorry we were a bit weak this year. Injuries and illness, you know how it is. Can't do anything about it. We'll give you a real game next season,' said Robbo with optimism and a surfeit of white lies, to the Wiveliscombe captain. Our secretary paused before revealing how easily he'd have got a first class degree in psychology if only he'd gone to university. 'Mind you, not many sides would have stopped you this afternoon. Lot of talent. Some lovely running. I liked the way you ran it whenever you had the chance.'

I know I didn't see all the game but Wivvy hadn't struck me that way at all. They simply left it all to their forwards, their big heaving, snorting, panting, guffawing, testicle-grabbing forwards.

The skipper had been just about to say what a load of spineless nancies we were and that if we hadn't been kicking the ball half-way to the Mendips, they'd have won 150-nil. Instead he savoured Robbo's sugared words. 'Yes, suppose we did look good. It's been like that every week. Not many sides are going to live with us this season.'

I trooped off with all the other players, from both teams. Our desperately recruited wing threequarter, badly in need of his glasses, was heading for the wrong dressing room and had to be recalled. He had hardly touched the ball during the game. His dog had noisily pined for him while fettered to a flag-post on the halfway line. Now master and terrier were reunited.

The Wivvy players were suddenly full of warm good humour and ribaldry. They were also without exception generous of spirit. We had our arms round each others' shoulders. I showered with the rest, inordinately proud of my gashed shin, and no longer self-conscious about my pale-bodied nudity.

I was one of the boys. You can't beat rugger at this kind of club level, we were all chorusing. Who the hell cared about the result, anyway? And how could you be expected to write knowledgeably about the great game unless you played it like a man?

I found myself stuck with rugby. It was a chummy arrangement. You had a drink and bandied words with the players during the week, commiserating with them on their discoloured half-closed eyes or ankles encased in plaster. On Saturdays, you ran, note-book in one hand when it wasn't raining, at the shoulder of the touch-judge – or occasionally onto the field, out of the sight of the referee, to determine who should be credited with the final touch of a pushover try.

Rugby players, I found, weren't sensitive in the way of their soccer counterparts. They even revelled in the gentle barb, and when some-one was praised he was mocked mercilessly. Not many of them were remotely match-fit but that was a sacred confidence one didn't share with the reader. In my reports, my initials were used after the heading, a rare accolade on a paper where any glimmer of the personality cult was vigorously discouraged. YEOVIL'S BATTERED HEROES HOLD OUT. . . By M.F. . . Or ALBION'S BACKS TOO FAST FOR SLUGGISH YEOVIL. . . By M.F. . .

With the Saturday afternoon job went various perks, apart from the augmented pay packet. One of the club officials was my dentist. He allowed me – and most of the team – to jump the queue. Unfortunately he cherished an old-fashioned, manly attitude towards physical pain. Rugby chaps were supposed to be used to taking a few knocks. They weren't expected to wince when he tugged in that clumsy, matter-of-fact way at a stubborn molar. And they were expected at the same time to exercise numbed jaws with esoteric discussion on last Saturday's match.

'Glad you don't waste your time watching Yeovil Town.'

I hadn't the heart to tell him that I did. Whenever there was no rugby, I would go to Huish for association football. The soccer managers would from time to time have morning coffee with us; they didn't have tiresome chores like training sessions to supervise then. Their players were part-timers.

Yeovil Town were renowned FA Cup fighters, of course. My father had taken me to see them play Sheffield Wednesday before the war. He'd taken his place on the terraces and positioned me on a beer crate in front of him. The smell of malt and hops wafted in from the local brewery then – and still did. Now Yeovil was actually at home to Sunderland from the first division in the fourth round. Everyone in the town wanted to see them. Yeovil 'A' had considerately cancelled their match.

Shopkeepers decked their shelves in Yeovil's colours of green and white; all of them wanted a mention in the *Gazette* on the strength of it. The players, who were glove cutters, lorry drivers and commercial travellers, managed to get a few days off work. They were apt to celebrate the fact by congregating at the convivial home of Nick, the club captain, who ran a pub only two hundred yards from the ground. I didn't see too much extra training being done, though the players demonstrated a flair for what a few years later would be called public relations. They posed, with wide, endearing unwordly grins for a succession of photographers. They held up rural lucky charms like rabbits' tails and affected to give themselves added muscle and stamina by drinking sherry with raw eggs.

Alec Stock, the manager, meanwhile got on with the more mundane aspects of his office. He helped cut the grass, checked the corner flags and made sure the emerald shirts had been properly washed. He was a man of quiet charm, not long out of the Army where he had been a captain. His father had been a Somerset miner; Alec, who had come to Yeovil by way of a grammar school, days as a bank clerk and then the officers' mess, had a controlled, nicely rounded voice which contrasted with the hearty and raucous vowels that emanated from a quaintly constructed directors' box, built on stilts and usually shrouded in cigar smoke.

My main concern was how I would see the game against Sunderland. All the tickets had long gone. The small, primitive press box, nothing more than a short, reserved row at the very top of the stand, would seat half a dozen reporters at the most. At least forty sports writers had applied for and received tickets. Many of them were due to sit on an exposed bench alongside the touchline. Some had applied too late.

If I had a problem, so had Ron who covered Yeovil Town's games for the *Gazette* and a score of other papers as well. He had the kind of orders for the historic match that promised to ensure him a long and affluent retirement – even at a guinea a time. But up in the top row of the stand there was just one telephone and only a remote chance of having another temporarily installed for the cup-tie.

'What are you doing on Saturday, Matt? Feel like doing a bit of phoning for me?'

We formulated our plan to give if not the whole nation then a goodly proportion of it a graphic account of the match more or less as it happened. The condition was that Ron would somehow obtain for me a messenger's pass.

Between us, the senior sports reporter and the eager junior, we worked it out. We knew at once there was no chance at all of my fighting my way every five minutes through thronged entrances and exits, and up between hundreds of knees in a sardine-like grandstand to the press row at the absolute, virtually inaccessible summit.

Ron had done a recce and had discovered in the woodwork at the back of the stand, over his right shoulder when he was in his cramped, seated position, a small hole. It was probably the cumulative result of age, decay and death-watch beetle. To us it was the passport to journalistic riches, however ephemeral.

The idea was for Ron to keep writing with furious resolve throughout the cup-tie and to pass batches of his pungent prose

149

through the hole, fastened securely to the end of a long piece of string. Then it would be lowered to me, conveniently stationed in the men's lavatories – 'very bloody conveniently' as Ron put it with an insensitive cackle. It was, we both agreed, a resourceful concept, based on split-second timing rather than fundamental hygiene. My No 1 typed a frighteningly long list of all his calls for the duration of the match, complete with times, destinations, telephone numbers and number of words. 'Going to have to rely on you to find a phone – you'll never get a call box.'

That was no serious problem. Mr Rousell, our family butcher, had his shop in the next street. I peered through his window and saw a black phone perched on the end of his meat slab. He was a football fan, I knew. This would be his vicarious way of keeping in touch with the tie as he served the weekend joints. The slab was spotless, the chops and cuts aligned in patterned rows. There was sawdust on the floor – and the imagined sound of whooping crowds already in my head. And only one hundred and fifty yards from what I already felt would be historic action on the pitch. Mr Rousell beamed and agreed. I bought some liver on the spot.

On the Saturday I reported to the ground (or, more accurately, to the urinals) as arranged at one o'clock. We were to have our rehearsal. Huish's surrounding streets, narrow and noisy, were already swaying with good-natured smalltown and rural humanity en masse. More than 17,000 supporters had somehow obtained tickets and the first of them were being filtered onto the railway sleepers that made up the bulk of the terracing. I wasn't at all sure so many people could physically squeeze into this quaint, sloping ground, itself claustrophobically wedged in by Douglas Seaton's sprawling garage, a tall Victorian infants' school and a hundred back gardens.

I stood, apprehensive and expectant, in the long, narrow lavatory. I made no effort to shift from my established position or to undo a trouser button. It brought me looks of curiosity, if not downright suspicion. Suddenly there was a bawling order from high above. A line of fans, bladders bursting from Bruttons, peered as one in the direction of the shout.

'Matt, are you down there? Here she comes!'

My eyes were glued to the small hole, which I could just make out. A folded bundle of yellowing copy paper began to appear, pushing and jerking its way out into the world like some wildlife reproductory function. Then it was gradually lowered on a piece of twine the thirty feet to my snatching fingers. It might

150

only be a rehearsal but I still undid the paper and read the words: 'I know most of my copy is piss-poor but do your best to catch it in time!'

With a glance of revulsion at the flowing trough at my feet, Ron's practical advice took on added meaning. I also chuckled. 'Everything went like a bomb,' I shouted up, using the wartime slang that was reluctant to go away.

'Be back ready at five minutes past three.' The cryptic conversation and the game-playing with a piece of string were way beyond the comprehension of the urinal's passing clientele.

There was still nearly two hours to go before kick-off. I wanted to absorb the atmosphere so barged my way back to the pavement outside the ground. Big green rosettes were being sold everywhere, along with special editions of the local evening papers. Every Sunday paper seemed to have its own poster:

SUNDAY PICTORIAL – Peter Wilson is here
NEWS OF THE WORLD – read our top man on the Huish heroes
SUNDAY DISPATCH – Yeovil's real inside story

So all the famous sports writers were here. My eyes glazed as they hovered on these newspaper bills. Would John Macadam, Roy Peskett and Clifford Webb, hallowed names all in my chosen first division of the Fourth Estate, really be down there on the touchline bench, notebooks and hip flasks at the ready?

A Gaumont British newsreel crew beavered away, capturing for posterity the pre-match bustle and lending glamour to the little town like never before. We watched with awe the way the cameraman in the belted raincoat, his equipment precariously perched on a battered tripod, kept whirring. Not many of us had seen a movie camera up close before. We felt we should be looking for John Mills and Robert Newton.

And who was that signing autographs? The Sunderland chairman, maybe, or an erstwhile celebrity of the football field someone had spotted? I edged forward like a wide-eyed schoolboy – and recognised the expansive moustache. Raymond Glendenning was the most famous commentator of his day. His camelhair coat contrasted with the functional drabness of Somerset working men out for a Saturday's sport. UP THE GLOVERS – RAYMOND GLENDENNING, he wrote on the covers of proferred programmes. Everyone called Yeovil the Glovers. Gloving was still the main industry. Dozens of housewives augmented the meagre family purse by stitching gloves on the kitchen table.

West Country people have always been pessimists by nature. 'Fog's comin' in fast. The ref'll need to have a look. May not even be able to kick-off.'

'Bollocks!' roared back a dozen other voices. You knew that if the ref had called off the game, he'd have been lynched on the spot.

I gazed up towards the quaint directors' box on stilts. It was hard to tell whether it was fog swirling in or cigar smoke swirling out. The businessmen of Yeovil liked to smoke cigars on special days. I could faintly hear the Silver Band. They had been in position on the centre circle since one o'clock. They couldn't wait to start their carefully rehearsed repertoire. At the moment it was the obligatory 'Colonel Bogey'.

And then suddenly, there they were: the Yeovil team. No-one quite knew from where; probably Nick's pub. They looked self-conscious in their shiny suits and wide turn-ups, frayed from rubbing against the ground. Under their coats were no-nonsense pullovers. Several of them, probably the country boys in the side, wore woollen gloves, knitted for Christmas. Apart from Nick, who was going bald, their hair had been parted with extra care. Sportsmen had always appeared to me to be preoccupied with partings and haircuts. No wonder Denis Compton's boyish waves were never off the hoardings. I remember thinking that the Yeovil players looked more like a bunch of gangling, shy supporters. They shuffled towards the official entrance. 'Good luck', everyone was shouting in the impassioned tones of a personal message. The weekly wage bill, I knew, was £65. It was money marvellously spent.

Ten minutes afterwards came Sunderland. Police had pushed back the crowds on both sides of the road to allow the coach to nose its way alongside the Huish ground. It was the best coach I had ever seen, with a big notice in the front window: SUNDERLAND FC. And to think I had once firmly believed that the rattling charabancs that took me on the Sunday School outings to Weymouth were the absolute zenith of luxury.

The team coach had come just the quarter of a mile from the Manor Hotel, where the players had been staying. They climbed out and I could see the difference straightaway. They were bigger and fitter – you could even detect it in the manner they jumped off the bottom step of the coach. Their suits were better cut than Yeovil's. Some of them had flashy footwear with pointed toes. They moved with a bit of a swagger: or did I just imagine it?

'There's Shack!' someone yelled. So it was. Len Shackleton paused on the steps of the coach and blinked in bewilderment at the density of the crowd. He was a small man with deep-set eyes and hair slammed back from a middle parting. There was no atmosphere quite like Roker Park. But the ambience that confronted him at Huish had an uninhibited rural intensity that made him uneasy.

The pundits had been saying that Shackleton, one of the game's most sophisticated ball artists, could beat Yeovil on his own. 'Ah, but only if he got a mind to!' was the Somerset retort. 'Old Bob Keeton cin look after he, all right.' Keeton was a commercial traveller from Torquay. I'm not sure what he was like as a salesman. As a tackler, unimpressed by reputations, he was lethal. Shack didn't know anything about Old Bob. He stopped to sign a programme on the way in. I moved forward, reporter's notebook already out of my pocket, to join the queue. Then I checked myself. Sports writers didn't do things like that.

Hundreds without tickets were left outside. The police promised to turn up their car radios when Glendenning's plummy commentary began. Meanwhile the Mayor arrived, chain of office dangling importantly. Most of the town council seemed to be following him, basking in publicity which had taken on global proportions; there had been telegrams of good luck from America and Australia. 'Now hope we can sell a few gloves over there,' was the instinctive response.

At a quarter to three, when I assumed both teams were changed and nervously bouncing footballs in the little dressing rooms, I saw Alec the player-manager. He was still in his brown suit, attempting to sort out a late administrative tangle with one of the officials. I had forgotten that Yeovil's players could change in two minutes flat. It was a practice they acquired from necessity through perilously late arrivals at away matches.

I was waiting at my post, very apprehensive, at five minutes past three. The first drop was quite impeccable. My hands were trembling as I unfastened the purple prose about the meaningless opening exchanges, and set off at an energetic trot for the butcher's. Mr Rousell paused in his duties, one hand steadying the stewing beef on the scales as he pointed knowingly, without a word, towards the phone. Ron's handwriting was clearer than I had expected. But the early copy gave my friendly butcher minimal information about the great game. I saw him nodding to himself, all the same, as I dictated the teams – with those famous names. . . Johnny Mapson, Jackie Robinson, Willie Watson, Shack. My teenage tongue savoured such sounds, investing them with an added verbal flourish in deference to their stature. I did my best with Dickie Dyke, Les Blizzard and Eric Bryant, but it wasn't quite the same.

My afternoon's work got harder, less romantic. Ron had been optimistic with his typed timetable of calls. It took longer than either of us had imagined to phone over the acceptable soccer clichés of the day. By half past three we were running late – and I was out of breath.

Often on my return to the ground, the lavatory was full and I had to take my turn before getting into position for the 'drop'. Several times, the copy was already dangling on the string two feet below the hole. I'd let out my self-conscious shout 'I'm waiting, Ron' and down would come the next batch. The stench of urine, influenced by the strong content of Bruttons, intensified. It was joyful relief to run close to the dressing rooms on my way back to Mr Rousell's. The aroma of liniment brought sweetness to the acrid recesses of my nostrils.

The butcher's shop always appeared to be full of housewives. 'You must hang on a minute and we'll know how they're doing,' the blue-aproned proprietor would tell them. All the time, the roars and groans of 17,000 delirious fans wafted not only into his doorway but into every doorway this side of the Mendips.

My presence took on increasing importance during my fourteen visits between five past three and ten to five. I fancy I became consumed with the sense of drama. Glendenning might be doing his well-enunciated stuff back on the police car radios – but I was dispensing the tidings to a shop full of housewives who showed no inclination to go home and prepare the tea.

By now I had become proficient at telescoping two calls into one for the same newspaper. Worse, I was presumptuously doing my best to improve Ron's narrative. I was slipping in eulogistic comments about Yeovil's prodigious skills in a game I hadn't yet seen. Suddenly I was an old-hand, on the end of a press box phone at Wembley. It was Wembley with the manly sniff of raw meat.

Twice on my charge back to the ground I squeezed for a moment or two into a passageway alongside Alec's tiny office, craning my neck to see my emerald-shirted heroes summoning up superhuman reserves.

Just once, when back in the lavatory, I had to lurch over the shoulders of a burly farmer with apparent prostate trouble. I snatched at and spilled my slip catch. It was calamitous. I gingerly extricated the soaked paper from the improvised trough, read what I could of the contents and memorised it. The facts, as relayed on Mr Rousell's phone, were suspect but the narrative fizzed with interest. Alec Stock was the scorer – and the shopful of housewives cheered. I said he hit it with his right foot and got it wrong. I took a chance and said the pass came from Ray Wright (all the passes seemed to come from him) and got it right.

The main thing was that I named the scorer correctly. I just didn't get names wrong. I had so much really to thank Cherry for.

There were two more scorers. But my lavatorial catching never wavered again and Ron's feverishly scrawled longhand was retained intact. Sunderland equalised and then Eric Bryant, who I used to see humping sacks of corn during my weekly village calls at Martock for the *Gazette*, won the tie to make history for a non-league club, in extra-time.

I don't know how I managed it but I saw snatches of the last ten minutes' play. Ron was never told. From my peephole in the passage-way near the manager's office, I saw the ecstatic crowd surge onto the pitch when they heard the whistle and thought it was the end instead of a free kick. Superintendent John Hanham pushed past the office to seize the microphone and plead as a loyal countryboy rather than with authoritarian fervour: 'Get back! Get back! It isn't over yet!'

Minutes later it was. And as I dictated my final dispatches, Mr Rousell was wiping his bloodied hands on his apron and chuckling. 'I told you that you didn't need to go to the match.' He was saying it to the remaining customers as if he had, with commercial fore-thought, provided an extra facility for the big day. He had certainly done well in clearing the slab. There were just two scrawny, tired-looking, fleshless lamb chops left, understandably ignored even by Yeovil's under-nourished, meat-rationed population. I bought them in gratitude – and also handed over two crisp one pound notes, given me by Ron to pass on for the loan of the phone.

My work was done; my raincoat pockets bulged with the fragmentary accounts of Yeovil's conquest of an illustrious team from the first division. I made my way back, this time to the dressing room, and staggered through the steam to join my Fleet Street peers as they chatted to the naked Yeovil players, leaning in ungainly postures against the side of the big bath. The players were smoking and drinking dark tea, poured from an enormous chipped, brown enamel teapot by the club's bald, paternal trainer.

'Where's Alec?' everyone was asking.

'Already changed and out counting the money. The manager's got to do the lot down here, old cocker,' said a lean home footballer with an incongruous London accent.

'Bloody stroll on – he deserves a rest after that lot.'

Everyone was having to shout above the din. I was overawed by my company. They were all here – and I didn't know which way to look. Should it be at the nude, hairy, magnificent Arthur and Ralph, faultless between them at full back? Or my other idols – Macadam, with his duffel coat and bristling RAF moustache, Peskett and Webb? The posters had said Peter Wilson was also here but I didn't see him.

There was a tap on the shoulder. It was Ron, looking like a triumphant scribe now possessing enough wherewithal to buy his own newspaper.

'Well done, son. No sweat, was it?'

'Bit late on one or two calls – but I caught up.'

I could see that Ron, with every justification, was pleased with the two thousand or so words he had scribbled, in meeting that dozen or more deadlines.

'Some good stuff there, Ron. Got all the drama of the occasion. You made me feel I saw every kick.' I meant most of it but I thought any more compliments would sound fulsome.

'Yeah, but well, it had it all. You can't go wrong with a game like that.' He contemplated his afternoon's endeavours and benumbed fingers. 'Yeah, I reckon I did pretty well.'

That was it. Yeovil, wage bill £65, were into the fifth round of the FA Cup. I walked back past the visitors' dressing room. The place was in silence, almost deserted. It seemed only right that I should go back to the urinal at the rear of the stand for a final pee. There was no jostling now. I took my time – it was a kind of ritual. I looked high up towards the top of the stand but it was too dark to see the hole.

Later that night there was to be a celebration dance in the Assembly Rooms and I would be paying my half-crown to get in. Before that, it was home by bike for tea.

My mother was unmoved by the drama and frivolities of the day. 'It's egg-in-nest, you'll like that,' she said. It was the high-tea meal, left over from the war years.

She knew I was due to phone someone else's reports from the family butcher's. But as she carefully eased the egg into its nest, she considered for the first time the size of the football crowd and the complications of the phoning operation. With perfunctory brevity I told her of an afternoon spent for the most part in the men's toilets at Huish.

Her reaction was immediate. She pushed the plate away from me as I was about to take my first mouthful.

'Before you do anything else, take some hot water from the kettle on the fire and thoroughly wash your hands.'

The tone of her postscript was even more reproachful. 'I just don't know what Mr Rousell thought of you.' For my part, I trusted that he never knew.

ELEVEN

Fouracre at Bay

BUZZ HAD GONE OFF to do his National Service and I
knew I'd be next. He looked in to see us when he was home
on leave. We joked about the precarious angle of his forage cap.
He held our attention as he told us how the RAF recruits went over
like ninepins when they were made to see the propaganda film about
VD. So it was back to the old subject. He explained to me how you
could pick up a prophylactic kit from the guardroom if you were
intent on an evening's promiscuity.

My paper wanted me to take deferment, completing my apprenticeship before going into the Services. Most of my direct contemporaries
in the village had already gone or were about to. This made me feel a
little uneasy. I wasn't quite sure why – probably a legacy from all the
wartime eavesdropping about army dodgers. But, for heaven's sake,
the war was over now. And as my managing director had asked:
'Wouldn't it make sense to be a fully qualified reporter by the time
you do your two years for your country?'

Frankly I couldn't see that I'd be qualified for anything, the
antiquated, if paternal, way I was being treated. So I supposed it
was really up to me to become as enterprising as I could as part of
my self-tuition, while augmenting my wages.

The misdemeanours of a Yeovil curate, well known to me –
our eyes met across the courtroom – were relayed to the *News of
the World*. This paper in those days filled its broadsheet pages with
almost self-parodied reports of sexual dalliances and indiscretions
under headlines like 'The Shame of the Curate who Offered his
Humbugs. . .' The *News of the World's* well tried, seldom flawed
technique was to ask the local correspondent to send the court case
in straight, verbatim fashion. It was left to the rewrite men in the
office to add the titillation.

It didn't occur to me to analyse what I was doing for a few pieces of silver. Was it fair, for instance, to bring added embarrassment to a wretched, menopausal curate? In the case of young provincial junior reporters like myself, it was more the excitement of trying to land a piece in a big-circulation Sunday paper. They were lousy payers, after all.

The Church was having a rough time from me. It was almost as if I was thirsting revengefully for all the boring sermons I had sat through as a choirboy.

A story of mine about a fifty-nine-year-old Yeovil clergyman who married a twenty-two-year-old Sunday school teacher against the wishes of her family made most of the national papers. The vicar had wanted the church doors locked during the service. But the Bishop of Bath and Wells, who had come to officiate, said that would never do. One of the big headlines said: WEST VICAR LOCKS CHURCH TO WED CHILD BRIDE.

By now I'd become adept at disguising from my elders at the *Gazette* my slightly more sensational activities in the broader service of the Fourth Estate. My own paper carried no more than a token paragraph. No ages were mentioned. There was no reference to the locked church. My tasteful treatment of the unconventional nuptials earned me commendation from on high within the office. 'You handled that most responsibly. We don't want any of that sob-sob rubbish in our columns, do we? We can leave that to those other. . . organs.'

My apparent sense of judgment continued to find favour. 'The newsprint position is improving – time for you to come up with one or two more ideas for a feature. Have you any up your sleeve?' I had.

Presumptuously I suggested a series on Strange Local Characters – one a week for as long as required. I could keep them going, I said with an air of bravado which might have been intended for the ears of Beaverbrook himself. My proposition was received with muted murmurs of enthusiasm. 'You could try one or two, for us to have a look at. No promises, mind you.'

Perhaps I would have stood a better chance, I ruminated, if it had been a series on Rural Deans I Have Known. . . or even. . . Drainage Schemes of the West. . .

At least the research appealed to me. It would give me the chance to find out about the witch who once lived at Ryme Intrinsica, the remains of whose house used to be pointed out to me in eerie respect by my father during our occasional bike rides around the local lanes. There was also old Nancy Cooper, who for years shuffled round the narrow streets of Odcombe and Montacute, begging for a penny or two, or a crust of bread. They said she wore a bundle of rags and always a sun bonnet; she was a tragic, once proud figure. She slept in hedgerows and spurned the workhouse. And there were Johnny and Carrie, whom I remembered personally from the prewar days when they came through the village in their delapidated pony and trap. Like Nancy before them, they often slept rough. Their mutual affection was touching. 'Have thee got a few rags, missis, fer I and poor Carrie who bain't very well?' Their mangy pony invariably looked on the point of death. Johnny and Carrie, old and leathery, may have been, too. But they used to hold hands as they traded oaths.

My plans for the series were cut short when the news diary was brought back into the reporters' room. 'You've got a job for tonight, Matt. Out at North Barrow.'

It was a time when blood sports had surfaced once more as a contentious issue. Labour, conscious that they had to shake themselves free from the stifling economic restrictions and the effects of a world food shortage, were ready for some renewed ideological fervour. Class distinction was the reliable standby of the Left. They turned on the hunting community. A Private Member's Bill was seeking to control those very country sports that the hunting-pink community held dear.

A meeting was being held at Barrow Court under the auspices of the British Field Sports Society. They were calling it a protest meeting – and intended coming up with a fiery resolution to oppose the Bill.

'Barrow's not too easy to get to at eight o'clock at night. But we ought to be there. There might be a bus.'

There was, for part of the way. It left Yeovil at a quarter to eight and dumped me at a deserted crossroads, according to the driver about a mile and a half from 'The Court'. I stepped down onto the country lane. The night was pitch black. For the next fifteen minutes I staggered almost drunkenly towards the faint lamplight from the nearest cottage. I knocked and asked for directions – at least I was on the right road. I also asked unrealistically, in view of the wind, for a box of matches. My agonising crawl continued, one foot gingerly planted in front of the other. If there was ever hope of the vaguest glimmer of light, the high hedges on each side of me reinforced the sheer blackness of the night. In my blindness, I could make my marginal movement only by keeping one hand against the grass verge.

A church clock was striking ten when with miraculous timing a solitary car came past. Its headlights revealed a driveway. When the car had gone, I found my box of matches. The faint flame flickered long enough for me to read 'Barrow Court'.

My traumatic orienteering under blindfold wasn't over. I veered repeatedly off the gravel driveway and crashed into bushes. At a different time, it would have been riotously funny. That night it was a scary experience. But, maybe with the instincts of a countryman, I reached the main door. It was ajar and I entered the oak-panelled hallway. I could hear voices from a room to my right. Even as I moved towards the door, people were beginning to come out. The meeting was over.

There were thirty or forty of them, I should say, that night at the home of Colonel Boles, the Member for the Wells Division. They all looked exactly alike: the tweeds they wore, the bristling moustaches, the slightly intimidating expressions. They stared suspiciously at me and I felt like a servant caught going through the guests' coat pockets.

'Em – excuse me, sir. Do you think I can have a word with Colonel Boles? I'm from the *Gazette*.'

They were far from convinced that I had the authority to be there at all. 'You shouldn't have been allowed in. This was a purely private meeting. Not for the Press.' The tweedy hunter turned to another tweedy hunter. 'Young fella here, Nigel, says he's from the newspapers. I've told him it was private. Don't you agree?'

He mostly certainly did. But I became consumed with the importance of my mission down the cavernous byways of North Barrow and knew that no reporter's reputation was judged favourably if he returned with an empty notebook. I repeated with added urgency: 'Can I possibly see the Colonel?' I paused and threw in an inspired postscript: 'A lot of my family are in his constituency.'

Such a deft conversational stroke confused them. They reluctantly went back into the room to find the host. There were whispers and glances back towards me in the doorway. Then the MP stalked over. I braced myself.

'Where do you say you're from?'

'The *Gazette*, sir. I expect you saw how much we gave to your speech at Glastonbury Town Hall last week.' Was my sycophancy going too far?

'A fine time to come, isn't it? We've just finished after two and a half hours. But in any case, it wasn't for the public. I don't know what your editor is thinking about, sending you to something that is so obviously a private meeting.'

'We thought it was in order to come. The meeting was advertised in the paper so we imagined it was open to anyone.'

Several of the tweedy hunters were taking a very sniffy view of my appearance. There was dead bracken stuck to my coat. I had a blue, dew-drop nose. But after such a tortuous trek, I had desperately summoned up reserves of persistence.

'And I'm sorry I'm so late getting here. It's been an awful journey. I seem to have walked halfway from Yeovil.' As I said it I knew it didn't sound at all like me.

The appeal to his better nature worked. He softened and said he could really see no reason why the local weekly paper shouldn't have a copy of the resolution just passed.

'Who are you sending it to?'

'Why, that Williams chap. Tom Williams, the Minister of Agriculture and Fisheries. . . And the Home Secretary, Chuter Ede. . . This is Captain Ashley. He was the chairman. Is there anything else we ought to tell him?'

The Captain said: 'I'll tell him what I said about you. That you earned the thanks of the whole West Country for the way you had taken a firm line at a time when too many MPs were. . . sitting on the fence, with a foot in both camps.'

Nothing like a good double cliché for the dear, old *Gazette*, I thought to myself as I committed the pearly pair to Pitmans. Which one would make the headline?

'The Socialists are turning this into a Party issue. We aren't. But I can tell you that they are going to lose a lot of country votes if they pursue this matter.' My notebook was beginning to fill.

The Member and his friends were sipping from their sherry glasses. I could see no sign of anything coming my way. Hospitality, I had discovered during my relatively brief career as a provincial journalist, was rarely extended to the Press. We lacked the status to be handed a drink from a cut glass. We were usually expected to enter by the tradesmen's entrance.

'And you can tell your readers, young man – hunting, field sports in general are for everyone. From nobility to the lowest man in the land. The Socialists bring Class into every argument. . .' He broke off.

'I don't suppose you're one of them, are you?'

I fidgeted. 'I haven't made up my mind yet.'

'Well, take my word for it. There is nothing privileged about hunting.' I was a good deal less than convinced.

In this same embracing of democracy, the Captain (gosh, I asked myself, was I in the presence of the whole British Army?) now spoke. 'There are no more buses tonight, young fella. How are you going to get home?'

I told him with complete honesty that I wasn't at all sure.

'Then Nigel can run you as far as Sherborne and you should be able to pick up a taxi from there.' Nigel's reaction made it clear he was none too enamoured with the suggestion that he should go out of his way for me. But I could hear him thinking – the General Election was coming up again in eighteen months' time and the local press had a role to play in putting those damned Reds in their place.

As Nigel dropped me off, he said: 'Remember what the Colonel told you. Hunting is a sport for everyone to enjoy. Put that in your report.'

The following month I had one of my rare free Saturdays. It gave me the chance for a long, solitary walk, high up across the Park, from where I would look down on the silent, ageless village I loved so much. During these walks I would philosophise in the immature, puzzled, inquisitive way of a teenager trying in vain to sort out his place and purpose in the universe.

I thought of my recent visit to Barrow Court and the patronising manner in which some of those British Field Sports people had treated me. It struck me more like a meeting of a diehard Conservative Association. Did life have to be carved up like this in tight, intractable compartments – with the Tories collectively bristling in the Big House and the resentful Socialists haranguing them from the public bar?

The Big House at East Coker was enclosed by the high hedge from where, as a small boy consumed with curiosity, I had once fallen almost at the feet of Queen Mary who was out strolling with her hosts.

In those prewar days the lilacs, tended by my father, were everywhere in full white or purple bloom. The gravel driveways, on the various levels, were free of weeds. The lawns were manicured, the grass banks trimmed and tidied by the week. Guests appeared through the Georgian windows and wandered idly to watch the goldfish in the ornate, circular pond on the lawn. The servants' quarters echoed to the clatter of a score of saucepan lids, or thick sensible scullery maids' shoes on the stone passageways. There was the scent of exotic shrubs drifting in, of rich wined sauces drifting out.

On this particular postwar Saturday, I knew that things were very different at Coker Court. The grass had become unkempt; the fishpond was overgrown and bereft of its pink, darting occupants. The servants' quarters, too, were virtually unpopulated. The fine Georgian house was cold.

Death duties had carried a cruel vengeance with them. Overnight almost, privilege had been turned to something approaching poverty. I wanted privately to approve of this whole evening-out process, which a Communist music teacher at our grammar school had once assured us was all there in the Bible ('Sermon on the Mount, boys – you should read it through and digest'). But my reaction reflected the feeling of parochial guilt. It wasn't easy to explain. My father might have been paid a paltry thirty-five shillings a week for working on the estate, and had his request for a Good Friday off questioned before being reluctantly granted. Yet I sensed that, within the rigid structures of a lingering feudal village of landowning grandeur and social elevation on the one hand and tacit serfdom on the other, there was a genuine affection shown towards those who laboured. And in its way, this affection was returned.

I continued climbing, beyond the reaches of the Court's outer fence and towards Spin Wood. I knew every stile and wicker-gate, most of them put in place by either my father or grandfather before him, that led into the wood. I knew every narrow track and moss-bound slope which was carpeted with bluebells in the Spring.

Spin Wood was my own treasure-island. The legends excited me: here and in Coker and Penn Wood across one or two more fields, where in the reign of George III the smugglers from the Dorset coast brought their booty to hide. And here the secret was discovered by a woodman from Pendomer. He was hacked to death. It was more than a legend. Joey Whetham, who farmed at Skinner's Hill, had told me his father knew the dead man's family. Another for my Strange Local Characters series, I mused. . .

My reverie was interrupted when I was still two hundred or so yards from the wood. I was conscious of yelping dogs and thudding hooves. I looked up – and the Hunt was bearing down on me.

First came the fox, bushy tail erect with fear, constantly changing direction, seeing me, momentarily half stopping as if in search of sanctuary, and then panting on in lessening expectation of survival.

Then the hounds: noses to the ground, blood already in the nostrils, oblivious to me.

After them the hunters, the horses not the riders. Fine chestnuts, bodies steaming in the crisp, winter air. There was animated instruction and anticipation from those in handsome hunting pink. They clearly thought the hounds were working well, cutting off the fox's hopes of cover in the woodland.

My own response was one of terror. Fifty or sixty hunters were charging at me. I suspect I was more frightened than the fox.

A voice from the head of the field bellowed at me. 'Get out of the way, lad!' Lad, indeed. The tone wasn't couched with concern for my safety. Rather was it a voice of indignation, from a man treating me as an irritant, getting in the way of the hounds – maybe even deflecting them. 'Out of the way, can't you!'

I saw a tree trunk and ran hard towards it. I pinned myself tight to the sturdy, protective bark and stayed motionless till the last chestnut had passed.

The strength of the hunting ritual was well known to me. I used to see pictures of the Hunt Ball Set in the society magazines, the men in their long scarlet tails and dance shoes that shone like a thoroughbred's coat in the sunlight, the girls in their taffeta dresses and expensive set perms. When the Hunt met outside the New Inn, I watched the stirrup cup passed round to good-looking side-saddled women, as if it were a fertility rite. The men's fleshy cheeks always seemed to match the scarlet of their jackets. I would gaze at the theatricality of the corporate wardrobe: the bowlers, the top hats, the polished riding boots. 'With a bit of luck, old chap, we should draw the first cover at Halstock. . .' The arcane language was a large part of the ritual.

And now here I was, trembling at the foot of an oak tree, almost run down by marauding madmen. . . and being curtly told to get out of the way.

That was the day I took my permanent stand against blood sports. It wasn't based quite so much on the morality of the chase as on the glint in the huntsmen's eyes. They didn't strike me as being very nice and civilised.

In the country we were inclined to grow up accepting the natural cruelty of nature and animal life, sympathetic to the hunting instincts of both animal and man. Take Albert and his two brothers. They were, like their father had been, rabbit-trappers from the village. They made their living from it. Once they cleared the overgrown

Channel island of Herm in a month. The three of them took their traps, snares and nets – not their ferrets. They killed six hundred rabbits a day. Albert and his brothers did their best to avoid cruelty but we accepted there had to be painful deaths from the snares. My own father and his sister were taught by my grandfather to spread a net out across the length of a field and to stake it to the ground. Then they had to drive the rabbits out from the hedgerows. The rabbits would become entangled in the netting or become trapped as they panicked. My father and his sister would run forward and pull their necks. It was done quickly, expertly. And it was part of country lore.

I didn't continue my walk that Saturday. After the Hunt had passed, the smell of the horses' sweat remained. It didn't appear to be much of a sport to me. Colonel Boles' unfurled words of democracy sounded oddly hollow.

On my way back down the hill I swung up again onto the spreading arm of my favourite sycamore. The smoke from the almshouse chimneys below were all wisping away in an identical direction, geometrically flawless as any piece of Busby Berkeley choreography. The parish was at peace and I wanted to cry with affection for my roots. I didn't understand too much of Eliot but, when he ruminated in verse about his beginning and end, end and beginning, was this – the view from the sycamore – what he was writing about?

Nothing would ever change in this distillation of serenity, I felt – and yet everything was. I wanted to see the Heneage lineage back at the Court against a background of clattering feet in the servants' hall. And yet I wanted a more just spread of wealth and opportunity. I wanted my beloved village always to be as tranquil as it was that Saturday in late afternoon. And at the same time I wanted the local lads back from the war to have their own cars as they chugged to Yeovil for well-paid jobs. What did I want? I wasn't sure.

Back in the cottage, Dad was poised to take down the football results, his Littlewoods coupon laid out on the table at his side. Mum was preparing high tea, egg-in-nest.

'Take off your dirty shoes and put on some slippers,' she said without looking at my feet. I stretched for my slippers from under the dresser. That was where all the shoes and slippers were always aligned, six or seven pairs, toes just visible, cherry blossom faces shining in the reflection of the oil lamp.

'Got some exciting news,' they told me. 'We heard in the post today and were going to keep it as a surprise. But we thought you'd like to know.'

I pondered the possibilities. 'Tell me.'

'They're putting the electric in before Christmas. Just think of that. No more having to read with your books propped against the lamp on the table.'

'What, in every room?' I asked naively.

'Right through the house. We didn't think it would ever happen.' They paused to note my delight. 'And they do say we'll be having a proper lavatory in before long. You know. . . a flush!'

Our eyes sparkled in triplicate. We suddenly felt we were terribly posh. But at the same time, I couldn't quite take it all in – not on a day when my mind had been in turmoil over the changes I wanted, those I didn't, and the opposites I wished to see at the same time.

Dad got three aways out of four. 'Accrington Stanley let me down again – I shouldn't mess around with the clubs from the north. You can't rely on them.' Another fortune, say fifteen bob, just missed.

By Monday's post came news of my call-up or, in the first place, my medical. There was much advice from the other reporters. 'You'll have to pee into a jam jar. Some blokes can't do it. Have plenty to drink before you go.'

My parents had qualms. 'Two years is a long time away. Will they keep your job open for you?' I said they would.

It wasn't for me so much two years away from the office as two years away from Coker. My attachment had grown more than I'd ever expected. We'd come through the war and Mr Cripps' clipped, austere sentences. We were emerging as defined individuals, yet part of a leisurely, good-natured community. We had our own vegetable gardens, neat, unpretentious front rooms – and our dignity. We didn't like to be told how to vote, or to move out of the way, by a humourless horseman who feared that his afternoon's sport might be ruined. We were prepared to leave Russia and America to the politicians.

Now National Service was plucking me from my cradle. Was it the break I needed? Should I stay away at the end of two years?

I drank well at breakfast and there were no problems at the medical. On the day I was due to report to RAF Padgate, the men arrived to put in the lavatory, 'the proper one with a flush'. My mother saw the irony of it. 'What a pity you won't be able to stay and do your business indoors now.' I said I thought Padgate would have reasonable amenities.

But I was reassured that the cottage now had electricity and a lav with a chain. It was some kind of civilised exit point for me.

My parents waved me off, just like they did when I started work. I could see my grandfather's bewhiskered face pressed against the window of his home across the road. I knew that Gran, huddled in her seat by the fire and her face twitching with the pain of the rheumatism that had emaciated her body, would be peering and waving her goodbye, too.

'Back in two years, Matthew. Back to Coker where you belong.'

I kissed Mother and Dad put a yellow rose in my buttonhole.

I wasn't quite sure what to say. 'I've sold the bike,' I told them, without explanation.